ON LIBERTY:

MAN
v.
THE
STATE

BY
MILTON MAYER

WITH
A CENTER DISCUSSION

PUBLISHED BY
THE CENTER FOR THE STUDY OF DEMOCRATIC INSTITUTIONS
SANTA BARBARA, CALIFORNIA

To the memory of
SCOTT BUCHANAN
who taught me that the questions
that can be answered are
not worth asking.

CONTENTS:

I   More Trial, More Error   7

II   Roll Call of the Wise Men   17

III   Sweeney Discovers Russia   27

IV   Alienable Rights   41

V   The Criminality of Conscience   57

VI   One Obnoxious Man   77

VII   E. Pluribus Einheit   91

VIII   Who Says There's a Fire?   109

IX   Hell or High Water   129

EPILOGUE: The Voices of the Young   144

I think we all have moral obligations to obey just laws. On the other hand, I think that we have moral obligations to disobey unjust laws because non-cooperation with evil is just as much a moral obligation as cooperation with good.

—REV. MARTIN LUTHER KING
   Nobel Laureate for Peace

An ordered society cannot exist if every man may determine which laws he will obey... that only "just" laws need be obeyed and that every man is free to determine for himself the question of "justness".

—LEWIS F. POWELL, JR.
   President
   The American Bar Association

CHAPTER

I

More Trial, More Error

The revolutions that shook the Western world in the middle of the Nineteenth Century were nothing more than a good shake-up. But they tumbled the royalists from their privileged perch and compelled them to accept the rule of law. For a hundred years thereafter, law, as the rampart of liberty, sustained the great expectations of Europe and America and the hopes of the rest of mankind. But in the middle of the Twentieth Century revolution struck again—this time *against* the rule of law as the *enemy* of liberty.

It struck in the "open" societies and the "closed"; to the distress of all patriots everywhere, its votaries disdain the distinction of "good" and "bad" states. It struck in Italy, India, Germany, Spain, and Chicago against what was lawful on those premises—and in Japan and Russia against lawful racism in America, in France against the lawful prosecution of Russia's poets, in London against the police of Paris. It struck all over the world against the lawful repression of "anarchy" in Berkeley and the lawful (even fraternal) rescue of Czechoslovakia from "counter-revolution." On the walls of the Sorbonne in May of 1968 was inscribed its universal slogan, *A bas l'état*—not this state or that one, but The State itself.

Most of its votaries are young, articulate, well educated. Not all of them. Mrs. Rosa Parks was none of these things when, on December 1, 1955, at the end of her day's low labor, she boarded the bus for home in Montgomery, Alabama, and, instead of going to the rear, as the law required of Negroes, sat at the front and was duly arrested, charged, and convicted by due process of law. Mrs. Parks overturned The State she happened to inhabit; old, inarticulate, and uneducated, she may not have thought, as she fell to her knees to pray, that what she was doing was overturning the rule of law itself. She said later that she decided to do what she did because her feet hurt.

The rule of law has disappointed its expectations. It has not mitigated the agonies of political association. Its full force applied on "the devil's warrant" of public necessity has been seen to be monstrous in the most benign societies. The mounting tension between Man and The State cries for principled consideration in the light of political experience unavailable to those who considered it in ages past.

Couch it how you will, in terms of liberty and authority, or rights and duties, or security and dissent, Man v. The State is what all the boiling issues all boil down (or up) to: democracy and dictatorship, public and private enterprise, self-reliance and social welfare, civil rights and individual determination, civil order and civil disobedience, national security and public protest, national defense and pacifism, public service and the right to strike, public sensibility and the right to publish, prosecution and the protection of the accused, criminal investigation and the right of privacy, "crime in the streets" and the police power, and the invasion of private and public property by break-in, sit-down, or blow-up against every vexation from dormitory hours to the war in Vietnam.

The most acute (if not the most vivid) illustration of this eyeball-to-eyeball confrontation is the persistent division in the United States Supreme Court, where crucial decisions are commonly made, and then unmade, with a shift of one Justice from one side to the other, by a "four-and-a-half to four-and-a-half" vote.[1] If, after all these millennia of political experience, the nine most highly elevated judges in a highly advanced society cannot discover the balance between the conflicting claims of the individual and organized society, we would seem to be doomed to live on in unrelieved twilight as a prelude to ineluctable darkness.

---

[1] The hyperbole may be read literally in the case of at least one of the eminent voters. "I am," former Justice Fortas wrote, "a man of the law. I have dedicated myself to uphold the law and to enforce its commands. I fully accept the principle that each of us is subject to the law . . . bound to obey . . . But if I had lived in Germany [under Hitler] or had been a Negro living in Birmingham . . . I hope I would have refused to wear an armband, to *Heil Hitler,* to submit to genocide . . . I hope I would have disobeyed the state law that said I might not enter the waiting room reserved for 'whites' . . . How can I reconcile my profound belief in obedience to law and my equally basic need to disobey *these* laws? Is there a principle, a code, a theory to which a man, with honor and integrity, may subscribe? Or is it all a matter of individual judgment? . . ."

The Justice then wrestled with the dilemma, and, it would appear, was thrown by it. He goes on to disallow "efforts to overthrow the government or to seize control of an area or parts of it by force, or by the use of violence to compel the government to grant a measure of autonomy to part of the population. These are programs of revolution. They are not in the same category as the program of reformers who—like Martin Luther King—seek changes within the established order." But he does not explain why, for example, the mass entrance into a waiting room reserved for "whites" is not an effort to seize control of an area by force, or how he would have refused to submit to genocide without using violence to compel the government to grant a measure of autonomy to part of its population. He would

9

In this twilight one tendency is clear: The State's power waxes and the individual's wanes. Even in the traditionally libertarian societies (and apart from social pressures) we are forbidden or compelled in a hundred ways unimaginable to our grandfathers—from compulsory vaccination and medical certification for a marriage license to building inspection and zoning regulations, from government standards for motor car manufacture to income and social security taxes. Peace-time conscription, restriction of travel, and self-exculpation of disloyalty are required of large sections of the American people, as are compulsory trade union membership and growing limitations upon the individual's liberty to hire employees, to choose his customers, or to sell or rent his home as he wishes.

"Defense" and "welfare" legislation cascades from every parliament in the world, regardless of the form of government. Under Communism, said Engels a century ago, The State would wither away at last; and a century later (after more than a half century of Communist rule in Russia) The State power, for good or

---

(it appears) have "spurned revolution in favor of seeking changes," but he doesn't tell us how this could have been managed "*within* the established order" of National Socialism.

"[The deliberate violation of law] is never justified in our nation where the law being violated is not itself the focus or target of the protest." The corollary would seem to be that such focus or target *does* justify deliberate violation of the law. But isn't each of us "subject to the law . . . bound to obey"? Apparently not. The justification is moral, not legal: the justified violator should . . . "admit the correctness of the state's action" and submit willingly to prosecution and punishment "if he is wrong or unsuccessful." (Hitler's Germany comes to mind again.) In any case the laws violated by the reformer King were not the focus or target of his protest; his entrance into waiting rooms, etc., was strictly symbolic. Apparently the reformer was a revolutionary.

And so on.

ill, is more pervasive and prolific under Communism than any ancient despot could have dreamed of, and The State apparatus more ponderous. *Collective* man may be freer from economic insecurity or hardship, but the individual who bothers to look beyond his own outstretched hand knows that he is paying a steadily increasing price in terms of his own independence of government controls.

Since the great age of national insecurity began some forty or fifty years ago, the "balancing" doctrine has grown increasingly popular in Congress, in the courts, and the law schools, insensibly replacing both the view that The State might not on any ground circumscribe certain individual prerogatives and the Holmesian criterion of "a clear and present danger" as the warrant for circumscription. In substance the current doctrine asserts that the ascription of absolute supremacy to one of the two contending goods—liberty or authority, freedom or security—annihilates the other; common sense, then, requires us to balance the two in the light of prevailing conditions to see how much of each we can preserve. (But there is ringing dissent from constitutionalists of the stature of Justice Hugo L. Black, who maintains that "the balancing approach assumes to legislators and judges more power than either the framers [of the Constitution] or I myself believe should be entrusted, without limitation, to any man or any group of men.")

The sticking point is the ambiguity of *prevailing conditions.* Under the ordinary conditions of ordinary life nearly all men live and die without coming into square conflict with the State. You and I are not Socrates on trial for his life, or Antigone facing death for having defied the unholy edict of the king, or even draft-card burners, or student militants, or a segregationist governor standing in the doorway of a university in Alabama. We pay our taxes, and otherwise conform to the laws, and there's the end of it. We grumble, of course, but the weight of The State is not onerous. What's it to you and me, *law-abiding citizens,* that a suspected murderer be uninformed of his right to be silent; or that a professional gambler have his telephone tapped or his boudoir "bugged"; or that a radical agitator be compelled to disclose his associations; or that the publisher of a raunchy book be punished unless he can prove its "social value"? You and I are not murderers or gamblers or agitators or publishers.

You and I are "little men," as such men call themselves in Germany. After the Second World War, I was arguing with one such there, who had been (and still was) a good Nazi; and I pointed out that the National Socialist dictatorship had deprived him and his fellow-Germans of their freedom of speech. His reply was as significant as it was ingenuous: "Who wants to make a speech?" Who wants to make a speech? Not many of us. The tenor of our lives under ordinary conditions does not require us to note (much less examine) the tension between man and The State. You and I do not have to make Patrick Henry's choice; and the few who feel that they do—well, they are the few. They are those over whom the Supreme Court splits. They are not, ordinarily, you and I.

It is the few who choose one or the other of the black-and-white extremes and, in doing so, point up the issues that escape the rest of us under ordinary conditions. They are not heroes; they may, indeed, be common criminals held for questioning. Or they may be "nonpolitical" individuals, like the soft-hearted farmer in southern Ohio who, before the American Civil War, let a runaway slave into his house and found himself aiding and abetting the theft of another man's property under the Dred Scott decision. Many were the nonpolitical farmers—or townsmen—then who came under the whole weight of The State. But that was long ago . . . or was it?

The issues that presently divide the courts, and convulse the world, are, in the last analysis, the issue that confronted the Ohio farmer. If he really means it, the man who says, "Better dead than red" is speaking the same language as Patrick Henry. The criminal who *takes the law into his own hands* is raising the same question as the priest who defies the Southern sheriff in a civil rights demonstration, or, for that matter, the Southern governor who defies the U.S. marshal in the second stage of the same demonstration: Does the law set the limits of liberty? What is there to keep the law from setting the limit at no liberty at all? Does the individual have rights that the law invades at *its* peril and not his? And if not, is not every state totalitarian in nature, however limited the actualization of its totalitarian nature under *prevailing conditions?*

The farmer who hid the runaway slave certainly found The State totalitarian. Of a sudden he no longer lived, as do most of us, in a world of comfortable grays: he either handed over the slave to his master or faced a terrible penalty. He had no time—and no impulse—to obey the law while he campaigned for its repeal ("within," as Justice Fortas would say, "the established order"). He had to choose then and there, with the runaway slave on his doorstep. And his choice, like that of the common criminal, was the destruction of The State in so far as he set himself above it. If (in addition to being human) he was philosophical, he was aware that his humane decision was nothing less than anarchy.

Anarchy. A few years ago a religious pacifist, who refused to pay taxes for military purposes, sued the United States to recover the tax which the Internal Revenue Service had seized under a warrant of distraint. His lawyer was arguing the case before the United States Court of Appeals and the presiding judge interrupted to say, "Counsel, is your client aware that if this Court holds for him, and permits him not to pay taxes because he objects to one of the purposes for which they are used, the Court itself will be laying the axe to the root of all established government?" The lawyer said that he supposed that his client was so aware, and the Court dismissed the suit.

The question, at bottom, is not whether there is more liberty now than formerly, or here than there; the question at bottom is the basis, if there is one to be found, upon which the citizen may be protected against The State, or the individual against society, without the danger of anarchy and the ruin of the community. The 18th Amendment was adopted in the interest of the general welfare of the American people, as the Congress and the legislatures of three-fourths of the states conceived the general welfare. It was overturned by lawbreakers in such numbers, raising the cry of liberty against tyranny, that the Congress and the legislatures yielded to anarchy and repealed the amendment. Had Prohibition impermissibly invaded a human right, and, if so, what right? What kind of right is it that validates the subversion of representative government? The duly constituted bodies that enacted and sustained the 18th Amendment located no such right; and the subsequent history of Prohibition indicated that there is no guidepost but trial and error, and more trial, and more error.

What is wanting is a line of demarcation between the conflicting claims of liberty and authority, not, to be sure, a line so clear that every imaginable case will fall untroubled on one side or the other; that would be too much to expect in human affairs. What is wanting, is a line that may be drawn with sufficient precision to indicate, when a given policy or practice of government is drawn across it, that the dosage of law may be too much for Man or too little for The State. The U. N. Declaration of Human Rights makes (or should we say "made"?) a stab at such demarcation, but some States (the U.S.A. among them) have rejected it and others have ratified it without any obvious disposition to abide by it. Without demarcation we would seem to be hard put to say what civil society is—much less the good society—and harder put to keep from swinging back and forth to the end of time in the see-saw turmoil symptomized by recent Supreme Court decisions.

The problem may be insoluble; which is not to say that it is a dead horse that will bear no beating. True, men, if they were angels, could live without government or be content with it (since it would be an angelic government); but they are not, and they cannot. But to rest on the proposition that the central problem of political life—the problem that *is* politics—is insoluble is to accept the counsel of despair. The problem deliquesces in academic limbo. At the very least, we ought to be bold enough to live with the anguish of its public discussion, understanding that the division of courts, parliaments, and peoples is not to be disposed of by slogans like "Nine Old Men" or "Impeach Earl Warren." The dead horse, for all its beating, is kicking up a fearful pandemonium all over the modern world.

CHAPTER

II

Roll Call of the Wise Men

To face the problem of Man v. The State is to recognize the uniform failure of political philosophy to solve it—or even to confront it. At the very beginning of recorded Western thought stands Plato's Socrates on trial for treason: "Men of Athens, I honor and love you, but I shall obey God rather than you . . . Either acquit me or not; but whichever you do, understand that I shall never alter my ways, not even if I have to die many times." After two thousand years the Athenian's defiance of The State remains the most eloquent of all testimonies to human liberty.

But hear the same Socrates a month later, in the death cell, rejecting his friends' arrangement for his escape: "A man must do what his city and his country order him; or he must change their views of what is just . . . He who disobeys [the laws] is thrice wrong; first because in disobeying [them] he is disobeying his parents; secondly because [they] are the authors of his education; thirdly because he has made an agreement with [them] that he will duly obey [their] commands."

Remember—these conflicting sentiments are not a tired old man's, but the formal handiwork of his great disciple, Plato, who uses Socrates as his dramatic mouthpiece. How shall we square the libertarianism of the *Apology* with the authoritarianism of the *Crito?* We shall not. The attempt has often been made, with the citation of Socrates' last speech in the *Crito* that he is "a victim, not of the laws but of men"; a vain attempt when we but consider that the laws are necessarily made and applied by men. Nor does Plato's pupil, Aristotle, serve us better maintaining, as he does, on the one hand, that "the state comes into existence [in order to furnish men with] the bare needs of life, and continues in existence for the sake of a good life," and, on the other, then conceding that "all belong to the state." Nor have any of the heirs of the Greeks succeeded in making themselves any clearer.[2]

The pantheon of liberty is of little service to us; Milton, Locke, and Mill all hang up on the horns of the dilemma. He whose *Areopagitica* rings with the cry, "Let [truth] and falsehood grapple . . . in a free and open encounter," is quick to seize the despised weapon of suppression when it comes to "popery, and open superstition, which as it extirpates all religions and civil supremacies, so itself should be extirpated." (This, in its

---

[2]The Thomist argument that The State is both an end in itself (as the common good) and a means to man's happiness (as a constitutive condition of that happiness) is a representative exercise. It leads to the cheerful conclusion that, given the perfectly just man and the perfectly just State, the conflict is only apparent, "the issue between individualism and totalitarianism false." "Unfortunately, neither men nor States are perfectly just . . ." M. J. Adler, "The Theory of Democracy," in *The Thomist,* 4 (1942), 313-328.

pristine glory, the argument latter-day Philistines direct against Communism.)

Milton denies liberty not only to Catholicism, but "that also which is impious or evil absolutely either against faith or manners no law can possibly permit, that intends not to unlaw itself." Off, then, to the death cell with Socrates on the finding of his judges that he is impious—or at least evil absolutely against prevailing faith or manners. Off, too, a bit later, with the advocate of Russian capitalism or American communism, whose offenses, whatever he has done, or whether he has *done* anything, self-evidently come under the "faith or manners" proscription.

John Locke, that ancestor direct of the American Declaration of Independence, would appear to exempt the generality of heretics and boors from the hemlock, but he is no less enthusiastic than Milton to extirpate the superstition of "popery": "These . . . who attribute unto the faithful, religious, and orthodox, that is, in plain terms, unto themselves, any peculiar privilege or power above other mortals, in civil concernments; or who upon pretense of religion do challenge any manner of authority over such as are not associated with them in their ecclesiastical communion, I say these have no right to be tolerated by the magistrate; as neither those that will not own and teach the duty of tolerating all men in matters of mere religion . . . That Church can have no right to be tolerated by the magistrate which is constituted upon such a bottom that all those who enter into it do thereby *ipso facto* deliver themselves up to the protection and service of another prince." Out of the shades of the not too remote days of Al Smith and even John F. Kennedy, emerges the spectre of "the Pope in the White House."

In his classic letter concerning toleration, Locke turns out to be no more tolerant than Milton of those whom the pious find impious: Beyond the pale are "those who deny the being of a God," on the ground that "promises, covenants, and oaths, which are the bonds of human society, can have no hold upon an atheist." (So, to the stocks or the stake, apparently, even those who reject oath-taking on the view that a person must always be truthful and cite Christ's injunction to "swear not at all.") Thinking, itself, comes under The State's control, though just how the control is to be administered Locke does not explain: "The taking away of God, though but even in thought, dissolves all." Religion, oddly, is the sole justification for intolerance: the atheist "can have no pretense of religion whereupon to challenge the principle of toleration."[3]

We are looking for liberty unfettered, and we find it cribbed, cabined, and confined by Plato and Aristotle in ancient days and by Milton and Locke between ancient days and our own. So we come to the paladin of Nineteenth Century Liberty, John Stuart Mill, who speaks to us in our own post-monarchical idiom. Mill sets the limit upon The State in terms so plain and so strong as to preserve his position almost unchallenged as the darling of the Twentieth Century libertarian:

---

[3]We are not concerned here with those prelacies, episcopacies, and puritanisms which by "liberty of conscience" mean their own; rather, with the hapless self-contradiction of those men and governments which mean to espouse universal liberty. Thus William Penn, in the Pennsylvania Charter of Privileges (1701) *both* repudiates the abridgement of freedom of conscience "as to Religious Profession and Worship" *and* protects whoever "shall confess and acknowledge One almighty God, the Creator, Upholder and Ruler of the World" against such abridgement; so the humble Quaker, like the Catholic Inquisitor and the Protestant Reformer, places the atheist and even the agnostic, outside the pale, and along with them, those true believers who deny the State the right to require confession and acknowledgement of belief.

. . . the sole end for which mankind are warranted, individually or collectively, in interfering with the liberty of action of any of their number, is self-protection . . . the only purpose for which power can be rightfully exercised over any member of a civilized community, against his will, is to prevent harm to others. His own good, either physical or moral, is not a sufficient warrant. He cannot rightfully be compelled to do or forbear because it will make him happier, because, in the opinion of others, to do so would be wise, or even right. These are good reasons for remonstrating with him, or reasoning with him, or persuading him, or entreating him, but not for compelling him, or visiting him with any evil in case he do otherwise.

Reading Mill (up to this point) we are satisfied that at last, after a few thousand years of beetle-browed bumbling, a political philosopher has appeared who is able to lay down a line of demarcation to which the lover of liberty may repair. The satisfaction is short-lived, however, for we have only to turn the page, a single page in the same essay, *On Liberty,* to find that the apparently water-tight doctrine is only the same old sieve:

There are also many positive acts for the benefit of others, which he may rightfully be compelled to perform; such as to give evidence in a court of justice; to bear his fair share in the common defense, or in any other joint work necessary to the interest of the society of which he enjoys the protection; and to perform certain acts of individual beneficence, such as saving a fellow-creature's life, or interposing to protect the defenseless against ill-usage, things which whenever it is obviously a man's duty to do, he may rightfully be made responsible to society for not doing. A person may cause evil to others not only by his actions but by his inaction, and in either case he is justly accountable to them for the injury.

We are looking for liberty unfettered, and here we are, back with Plato, Aristotle, Locke, and Milton; or further back still. On one page The State may prevent my doing harm to others—that much, and no more; on the next there are "certain acts of individual beneficence" which The State may compel me to perform. A woman screams on the street in the night—and I rush (unarmed as I am) to her aid or suffer The State's penalty for remaining in my room. A lynch-mob passing my house . . . a man crying for help in a flaming building or on a storm-swept sea . . . a bully (bigger than I) ill-using a defenseless man (of my own small size), and I must plunge in, wade in, dive in—at the peril of my own life—or "rightfully be made responsible to society." My benevolence is not mine at all; the law drives me to it; I am a conscript hero. A marvelous doctrine, this, which I have seen applied (though mildly) under a Communist or fascist tyranny, but never in a society that was even fairly free.

And that dreadful limitation of liberty is not the last of Mill's. He urges nothing less than despotism (the very term is his) as "a legitimate mode of government in dealing with barbarians, provided the end be their improvement, and the means justified by actually effecting that end. Liberty, as a principle, has no application to any state of things anterior to the time when mankind has become capable of being improved by free and equal discussion. Until then, there is nothing for them but implicit obedience to an Akbar or a Charlemagne, if they are so fortunate to find one." Of whom are we speaking here? Over whom are we licensed to practice despotism? Why, "barbarians." But who are the barbarians? Clearly the subjects of European imperialism, Kipling's "lesser breeds without the law"; to be enslaved first, then to be improved, and then, but only then, liberated when the imperial power decides that they are civilized. But one man's civilization is another man's barbarism. Gandhi was a barbarian ("a half-naked fakir," Winston Churchill called him). So were the Irish, and the Indonesians, the Algerians, and, come to think of it, the American colonists (and in Lord North's words). The whites of Southern Rhodesia presently regard the blacks as barbarians—but the United Nations found the whites barbaric and imposed sanctions on them. And which are the barbarians in Mississippi who are not yet "capable of being improved by free and equal discussion?" Only stamp a man, or a people, or a nation, or a party, or a person a barbarian and you have legitimized his enslavement.

Abraham Lincoln hated slavery with his whole heart, excoriated it, and asserted that, rather than accept the view that all men are created equal except Negroes, he would "prefer emigrating to some country where they make no pretense of loving liberty—to Russia, for instance, where despotism can be taken pure, and without the base alloy of hypocrisy." Hence, if ever, was the lover of human liberty above all other goods. But as late as the summer of 1862, resisting Greeley's demand for emancipation of the slaves, Lincoln wrote, "If there be those who would not save the Union unless they could at the same time *destroy* slavery, I do not agree with them. . . . If I could save the Union without freeing *any* slave, I would do it; and if I could save it by freeing *all* the slaves, I would do it; and if I could save it by freeing some and leaving others alone, I would also do that. What I do about slavery, and the colored race, I do because it helps to save the Union." These are the words of (as he proved to be) "the great emancipator," *balancing* liberty and authority, freedom and security, man and The State, and coming down for "The Union."

The Union was, in the military event, the majority. The slaveholders were an important minority, whose strong opposition was overcome not by the superior morality of the abolitionists, but by the big battalions. But the runaway slave—the supplicant at the Ohio farmer's door—was neither an important minority nor a strong opposition. Who pleads his liberty, and on what rationale? He stands there still, done down by the wisdom that runs all the way from ancient Athens to the Nineteenth Century White House. He stands there still, and he fares no better than he ever did: "The genius of the American system," says Walter Lippmann, "is that it limits all power—including the power of the minority . . . The American idea of a democratic decision has always been that important minorities must not be coerced. When there is strong opposition, it is neither wise nor practical to force a decision." If only the runaway hadn't been unimportant and weak—or if only he had been patient enough to wait a century until he had accumulated Black Power and become an important minority and a strong opposition, the democratic genius might have stayed its hand in the face of his importance and his strength instead of dragging him away from the farmer's door and returning him to his master.

We search for an unassailable rationale for the unfetterable rights of man, and the wisdom of the wise fails us from age to age. We turn perforce to the eternal

24

wisdom of the Scriptures. Christ's reply to the Pharisee's question, Whose was the tribute money? has always been cited (and always will be, no doubt) on both sides of the case. But he seems to have made it with intent to frustrate those who meant to entrap him, and compel him to say either "Caesar" or "God," for we read that he made it *perceiving their wickedness* in asking it. True, His kingdom, he said, was not of this world; but his apostles formed a congregation of men who (though their kingdom was elsewhere) were men, and, as men, men of this world and members of one of its States. To The Book, then, we resort, and, sure enough, Peter tells us how the dilemma is to be resolved: "We must obey God rather than men" (and the other apostles all said so with him.) But we proceed from *Acts* to *Romans*—again a passage of only a few pages—and find Paul saying, "Let every soul be subject unto the higher powers. For there is no power but of God: the powers that be are ordained of God . . . For rulers are not a terror to good works, but to the evil." Lackaday. If we would pay Paul the respect due him, we must rob Peter. But we shall not get off as easily as that, if we but proceed to 1 Peter 2:13, where *Peter* robs Peter and says, "Submit yourselves to every ordinance of men for the Lord's sake; whether it be to the king, as supreme; or unto governors, as unto them that are sent by him for the punishment of evildoers and for the praise of them that do well."

Little wonder that modern philosophers and politicians are tempted to avoid the question altogether. Their difficulty, and ours, is that they do not say that they have no answer but, like heaven and earth before them, go on answering both ways. If there is one contemporary American platitude that pleases us more than another,

25

it is that *there* man exists for The State while *here* The State exists for man. Breathes there an American with soul so dead who ever to himself said otherwise? And was not John F. Kennedy a great American patriot? Who was it, then, who said so imperishably, "Ask not what your country can do for you: ask, rather, what you can do for your country"? And what people was it that responded, and still responds, so fervently to those words which on second thought (or first) say something very like the contradiction of the received American platitude? Mr. Kennedy's hagiographic utterance could have been just as hagiographically uttered by Adolph Hitler or Josef Stalin.

Are we then demanding an absolute where none is possible and no reasonable man will ever find one? No, there is one possible, and reasonable men have found it. The absolute is autocracy, the whole denial of liberty, and it has been advanced again and again, in modern times as in ancient (and not always by madmen). Thomas Hobbes in Seventeenth Century England will do for the rest. "The commands of them that have the right to command," says the author of *Leviathan,* "are not by their subjects to be censured nor disputed." If this is where the quest for certainty leads us—to absolute monarchy and the divine right of kings to make the law and live above it—we say we will every man-jack of us choose uncertainty and go on playing it by ear. A thousand times rather the pitfall than the pit. Are we sure?

CHAPTER
III
Sweeney Discovers Russia

There are social scientists, no less than rulers and philosophers of rule, who look upon The State (or the society) as a "social organism" and study it as such and on it postulate a politics. The philology of the expression is itself suggestive: "organism" is not a collective noun and has no way of denoting an aggregation of *individuals*. But it has a kind of historical sanction in the most (as well as the least) reputable historical contexts. Libertarianism no less than despotism invokes the authority of a people—the Declaration's "one people," Hitler's *"das Volk,"* the U.N. Charter's "self-determination of *peoples"*—as if the whole number of persons dwelling in a given geographic area had an organic identity and no other.

But an organism is a self-subsistent entity, its "members" wholly dependent upon its function, devoted to its maintenance, and dispensable (when necessary) to its survival. The sociological usage of the term at once conjures up the totalitarian State, the "ant-heap" whose members, though they are physically individuated, act like subservient parts of a whole. We libertarians reject the analogue and insist that The State is an association of organisms and not itself one. The social organism school has, however, a long line of weighty forebears beginning with Aristotle: "The whole is necessarily prior to the part; for example, if the body be destroyed, there will be no foot or hand, except in an equivocal sense, as we might speak of a stone hand. . . . The proof that The State is a creation of nature and prior to the individual is that the individual, when isolated, is not self-sufficing; and therefore he is like a part in relation to the whole."[4]

If we agree that The State is a creation of nature, and that man is therefore born a political animal, we seem to be accepting the Aristotelian priority which holds that the individual needs organized society as the part needs the whole, but that organized society does not need the individual. But our troubles have only begun, for the same philosopher who calls The State natural (and man by nature political) praises him "who first founded The State" as "the greatest of benefactors"; as if to say that The State is an artifact and that men, however well or badly they may have lived, once lived without the "whole" of which they are "parts."

If man is *by nature* political, it is plain that he cannot realize his nature, i.e., fully be a man, without The State; without it, says Aristotle, he is not a man but

---

[4]In 1967 the Prime Minister of Greece, Col. George Papadopoulos, informed an interviewer that his military dictatorship emulated Aristotle's theory "that The State can intervene in regulating the individual."

"a beast or a god." (Score one for the social organism.) The case is classically argued in political philosophy on the hypothesis of a "state of nature" chronologically antecedent to the state of society. The supposition that man in the state of nature was free—or freer than he is in society—is traditionally dismissed as romantic. For the legendary "noble savage," life (according to Hobbes) was "nasty, brutish, and short," with (as Locke put it) every man's hand raised against every other. To escape these "inconveniences," men abandoned the state of nature and society came into being. Men might be less free—less free to take and to kill, but also less free to be taken from and be killed. Freedom with absolute insecurity of life and property is illusory. Score again for the social organism . . . and abandon altogether the liberty of the "part" against the "whole"?

Hung up on the concept of the state of nature—a state for which there is no evidence archaeological or historical—lovers of liberty no less than its enemies have contributed their mite to its reduction. Jean Jacques Rousseau searched out an imaginary "original" of society in the absolute but fatal freedom of pre-social conditions. He decided that there must have been "one occasion," a celebrated, mythical moment at which free men in the state of nature assembled to form a social compact and freely voted, every one of them, to "[alienate] all his rights to the whole community," putting "his person and all his power in common under the supreme direction of the general will" in which "each member [is] an indivisible part of the whole."

Here again, of course, we have the part-and-whole doctrine of Aristotle, just as, in a statement of Abraham Lincoln's, we have the Aristotelian analogy of the hand and the body. "By general law," said Lincoln at the height of the Civil War, "life and limb must be protected, yet often a limb must be amputated to save a life; but a life is never wisely given to save a limb." So, too, the Genevan friend of liberty lays the foundations for universal slavery in the surrender of every man's "person and all his power" to the general will of that artificial whole, the people.

Rousseau's "one occasion," on which that surrender was made, is no more than a gloss on the argument of Socrates in the *Crito:* He must not disobey the law of Athens, under which he is sentenced to die, because when he came of age he had been free to emigrate and take his goods with him, and having had the experience of Athens' laws, he "chose" to remain an Athenian and thereby "entered into an implied contract that he will do as [the laws of Athens] command him." Here the sovereign individual has exercised his sovereign choice to abdicate his sovereign liberty—in theory. The actuality is something else altogether. Habit conspires with necessity to keep almost all men where they are; neither are they conscious of Rousseau's "one occasion," or of any Socratic commitment (though they may approve of the present laws generally) to obey whatever laws may be enacted in the future.

In and of itself majority rule—which is all Rousseau's "general will" comes to—does not in the least protect the liberty of the minority. The "tyranny of the majority" is as old in political theory as majority rule itself, and as familiar in practice. Common sense conspires with common experience to reject the doctrine that the common good is ipso facto *my* good, the general welfare ipso facto the particular; we want to know more about *my* participation in it before we accept it; still less are we enthusiastic about "the greatest good of the greatest number." What about the smaller number? (The Negroes of the United States are 11% of their country's population, and the Jews of Nazi Germany were 1%.) What about the smallest number? What about one man? Mill argues that if all the members of the State are on one side, and Socrates alone on the other, The State still needs to hear Socrates. But the prospect is poor that it will—as poor as the prospect that the Russians will hear the single anti-Communist in their midst or the Americans the single Communist.

"There is," the fourth President of the United States wrote to the fifth, "no maxim, in my opinion, which is more liable to be misapplied, and which, therefore, more needs elucidation, than the current one, that the interest of the majority is the political standard of right and wrong. Taking the word *'interest'* as synonymous with *'ultimate happiness,'* in which sense it is qualified with every necessary moral ingredient, the proposition is no doubt true. But taking it in the popular sense, as referring to immediate augmentation of property and wealth, nothing could be more false. In the latter sense, it would be the interest of the majority in every community to despoil and enslave the minority of individuals."

Maxim Gorky drags the skeleton from the democratic closet when he says, "The people is the enemy of the man." Consider, if you will, that I am the only Druid in a State whose whole population, numbering one hundred, consists of fifty Methodists, forty-nine Baptists, and me. My religious faith and practice are a scandal of horrendous proportions, and there are a dozen charges on which I can be had up; "disturbing the peace" is one of them. Whether I have disturbed the peace is determined by a jury whose peace is disturbed by my very existence. They convict me, on Milton's permissible grounds as "evil absolutely against faith and manners," or on Locke's complaint that I am an atheist ("though but even in thought"), or on Mill's that I do not perform "certain acts of individual beneficence"; and so I have had my day in court and the services of the greatest of all solicitors of liberty. The jury then votes the penalty, as was the case in ancient Athens and in the hypothetical State I speak of. The Methodists propose hanging, the Baptists electrocution, and the campaign between them is carried on in the best two-party tradition of democracy, with a public fully informed. The vote, however, is along strict party lines; the fifty Methodists prevail; and democratic justice is done the one Druid.

The hyperbole may be suggestive. Arguing for the adoption of the Constitution, the authors of *The Federalist* reported that "complaints are everywhere heard from our most considerate and virtuous citizens, equally the friends of public and private faith, and of public and personal liberty, that our governments are too unstable, that the public good is disregarded in the conflict of rival parties, and that measures are too often decided, not according to the rules of justice and the rights of the minor party, but by the superior force of an interested and overbearing majority. However anxiously we may wish that these complaints had no foundation, the evidence of known facts will not permit us to deny that they are in some degree true." The remedy, it was argued, lay in the selectivity and restraint inherent in the representative (or republican) government the new Constitution envisaged, and in the great variety of parties (or factions, or interests) in the larger Union in contrast with the individual states. But the trend of succeeding times, impelled by technological advances in communication, and especially in public opinion polling, has been away from variety and, concomitantly, in the effective direction of direct (or, perhaps, "instant") democracy. The Federalists, now perhaps more than then, are helpless to guarantee *my* liberty against "an interested and overbearing majority."

Nor does representative government serve me any better. So, far from being a guarantee, it is itself a denial of my liberty: it does not represent *me*—it represents *us*. If I am one of the 49.99% who voted against "my" representative, and he wins by 50.01% of the vote, I may be unrepresented. And if the minority to which I belong shrinks to 1% or less, my prospect of representation is remote indeed. I am supposed to have given my consent to a government whose sole legitimization is the Declaration's "consent of the governed." But here I am governed without my consent under laws enacted by a legislator I opposed; and I am to subside in the cold comfort of the supposition that what I consented to was, not this law or that, but representative government. But it is precisely this law, or that, that limits or destroys my liberty.

We shall be reminded that the basic charter of a representative government provides explicit safeguards of the person against "the people." But these safeguards, even when they are enshrined in a constitution, have been known to be meaningless; while the best protected person in the world is probably the Englishman, who has no constitution at all. The Bill of Rights was amended into the United States Constitution. It can be amended out by the same process. Or it can be interpreted out by the courts.[5] Or it can effectively be suspended by the executive and its suspension validated by the courts on the ground of national emergency even without martial law.[6] Or it can be overridden by a government which has managed to render legislature and judiciary supine, as in Nazi Germany or the Soviet Union or Franco Spain. Or it can be nullified by popular passion which The State power itself (above all in a democracy) may be incapable of resisting.[7]

We shall be told that these are hollow terrors all; that we do not look to Communist Russia or Nazi Germany to discover where liberty is or whether it can be guaranteed against the tyranny of the many or the one; that we are splitting hairs (the hairs of the dead horse we are beating) with our medieval excursions into the metaphysics of whole and part and the mythology of the state of nature; that government is sufficiently re-

---

[5]"The meaning of due process and the content of terms like liberty are not revealed in the Constitution," Justice Felix Frankfurter wrote. "It is the justices who make the meaning. They read into the neutral language of the Constitution their own economic and social views. . . . Let us face the fact that five justices of the [United States] Supreme Court are molders of policy."

---

[6]*V.,* for example, the case of the "Nisei" of the United States West Coast; p. 55.

---

[7]A popular passion like anti-communism can starve a man by refusing him a job, as it did in the "blacklist" cases of the McCarthy period of the 1950's. In the same period the popular passion of anti-Nazism silenced the late George Lincoln Rockwell in New York City by refusing him a public platform, and in the 1968 Presidential election the popular passion of anti-segregation deprived the third party candidate, George Wallace, of the use of that same city's only arena large enough to accommodate his audience. In 1969 the popular passion for law-and-order deprived the radical Students for a Democratic Society of a campus for their summer convention. (They were refused by thirty-seven colleges and universities—including Harvard.)

sponsive and liberty sufficiently secure in the good society, and that we have got to get down to cases closer home than the Druids if we would persuade the reader otherwise. Closer home, then.

It is Saturday evening and, being a good, clean American, or, at least, a clean one, I am running the water for my weekly bath. While it runs, I sit in the sitting room of my home. (Who but the most egregious of despots would deny that a man's home is his castle?) Being an artistic, as well as a clean American, I am strumming on my electric guitar; the melody, naturally, is, *Home on the Range.* There is a hard knock at the door, as of wood on wood. I unlock the lock of my castle, and Officer Sweeney walks in without so much as a by-my-leave.

Now Officer Sweeney and I are old friends; but his demeanor tonight is such that I ask myself whether he might not have broken down the door had I declined to unlock it.

"Turn off that water," says Officer Sweeney, "and get your boots on and report for duty at the corner of Pleasant and Prospect at once. The town is on fire, and the fire is out of control, and we've got to save water and have help."

"Now, see here, Sweeney, old boy," I say, still strumming my guitar, "are you telling me, an American citizen, that I cannot sit in my own house, disturbing nobody, *and take a bath* on Saturday night?"

"That's what I'm telling you," says Officer Sweeney, reaching for his club.

"And," I go on, laying my guitar aside and reaching for my copy of the United States Constitution, "are you telling me that this is America—or are you telling me that this is Russia?"

35

"I'm telling you," says Officer Sweeney, "that the mayor has proclaimed martial law."

"And *I'm* telling *you,* martial law, smartial law, the Constitution is the supreme law of the land and it says something here about search and seizure and the privacy of my home and—."

"—And I'm telling you," says Officer Sweeney, advancing upon me and brandishing his club, "to turn off that water and get going to Pleasant and Prospect—or else."

"Or else what?" I say, brandishing my Constitution, but Officer Sweeney has retired, and not in confusion either, and is heard banging at the portal of the castle next door.

The fire is extinguished, the city is saved, and the citizens, including me, are told by mayoral proclamation that they have done their duty, except for a few laggards who refused to cooperate and will be punished to the full extent of the law (martial), which is "repealed" in the same way it was "enacted," namely, by mayoral fiat, or tyranny.

My electric guitar gathers dust for a week as I meditate my Constitutional rights (apparently dissolved at the whim of the mayor, against whom I voted at the last election, and who got in by gerrymandering three wards) and my un-Constitutional duty to save the city in which (to put it plainly) I have no interest, and away from which my castle lies at a sufficient distance so as to be unendangered by fire.

It is Saturday night again, and I am running the water and, for the first time since the fire, trying *Home on the Range* on my guitar. There is a gentle rap on the door, as of knuckle on wood, and I unlock my castle, and there stands Officer Sweeney, un-uniformed and unarmed. "May I come in?" he says. "Of course," say I. He comes in and says, "Professor, I told the boys down at the Precinct House that you have a copy of the Constitution, and they want to know if there is anything we can do about wages and hours and working conditions."

"Well," I say, "it does say that involuntary servitude is prohibited. Are you serving involuntarily?"

"To be perfectly frank and tell you the honest truth," he says, "we are. We were going to go on strike, that's how bad it is, and the Governor sent a telegram saying he'd have us in jail—imagine! loyal and honest policemen—if we struck for better hours and wages and working conditions. Can they do that to us? Can they *make* us work if we don't want to? It's slavery, that's what it is."

"Call it what you want," I say, "and be it what it may, policemen can't strike."

"Why," says Officer Sweeney, "it sounds like—"

"—Russia," I say. "And," I go on, "you may remember when you dropped in last Saturday night—"

"I'm sorry about that," says Officer Sweeney, "but the city was on fire and it had to be saved."

"Tonight," I say, "the city is crawling with criminals and you, as a policeman, are its only hope of salvation."

Sweeney has become pensive. I strum softly.

"Professor," he says, "you know my boy Martin."

"Since he was—" I say.

"—Well," says Officer Sweeney, "they put him into the Army and he doesn't like it. He says they are going to ship him off to Vietnam, and he might get shot. He's going to resign."

"Oh, no, he isn't," I say.

"He'll just quit," says Sweeney. "He won't go."

"And if he quits," I say, "he will certainly be shot, or otherwise punished."

"By the Russians?" says Officer Sweeney.

"No," I say, "by the Americans. Soldiers can't quit any more than policemen can strike."

"But that," says Officer Sweeney, reaching for my copy of the Constitution, "is involuntary servitude."

"Just as mine was last Saturday night."

"I never thought of that," says Sweeney. "What about those Constitutional rights you were talking about. Are they all suspended? It sounds like Russia."

"It sounds," I explain, "like Russia and every other country that ever was or ever will be, including the Scandinavian, the Medes, and the Persians. The rights are not actually suspended—they're simply, well, put on ice until the emergency blows over. You know—the safety of The State, or the city—the national security—a clear and present danger—that sort of thing."

"And who decides that there's an emergency?" says Officer Sweeney.

"The Government," I say.

"But," says Officer Sweeney, "it's the Government that we're up against in the first place, and now it's the Government that decides there's an emergency that won't let us argue with the Government. Do you call that fair?"

"You don't call it fair or unfair. You call it emergency."

"And how long does the emergency last?"

"As long as the Government says it lasts. In Nazi Germany it lasted as long as the Nazi Government lasted—twelve years. In Communist Russia Lenin's five years of 'war communism' goes on and on. We're nothing like Nazi Germany or Communist Russia, of course, but some of the national emergency powers the President asked (and Congress granted) in 1917 are still in effect, and so are some others from the Nazi emergency of 1940 and the Korean emergency of 1950."

"So," says Sweeney, "we have to wait for our rights until—"

"—Until The State decides that their exercise does not jeopardize the safety and security of The State," I say, strumming softly, "and that, old friend, is exactly what I had to do last Saturday night when all I wanted to do was take a bath." And *that* stops Officer Sweeney at last.

Had I not been a week late for my bath already, I'd have told Sweeney about Milligan, whose first name, as every law student knows, is Ex Parte. Milligan, a civilian, was arrested in Indiana by order of the military commandant on October 5, 1864. A military court (established by authority of President Lincoln) sentenced him to be hanged by a military commission for inciting insurrection. A year later the United States Supreme Court freed him in one of the "landmark" cases of American history. "No doctrine ever involving more pernicious consequences," said the Court, "was ever invented by the wit of man than that any of [the Constitution's] provisions can be suspended during any of the great exigencies of government. Such a doctrine leads directly to anarchy or despotism. . . ."

If, the Court went on, the commander of an armed force in time of war has the power to suspend all civil rights and subject citizens to the rule of *his will* [italics the Court's] and cannot be restrained except by his superior officer, or the President as Commander-in-Chief, then "republican government is a failure, and there is an end of liberty regulated by law. Martial law, established on such a basis, destroys every guarantee of the Constitution and effectually renders the 'military independent of and superior to the civil power'—the attempt to do which by the king of Great Britain was deemed by our fathers such an offense that they assigned it to the world as one of the causes which impelled them to declare their independence. Civil liberty and this kind of martial law cannot endure together; the antagonism is irreconcilable; and in the conflict one or the other must perish."

CHAPTER
IV
Alienable Rights

Plainly, what one man calls justice, another calls expropriation; and one man's security is another man's slavery; and one man's liberty is another's anarchy. And it is just as plain that there is no great point in moving at all if we do not know where we want to go. In practical matters the objective is the ruling principle of action. If our inexorable objective, or ideal, is the maximization of the State's security *or* the maximization of the individual's liberty, we shall never know how to make our public or private decisions as legislators, judges, or citizens, unless we approach the problem in the best dialectic tradition by projecting it to its two contradictory extremes and seeing what happens to us.

We have already seen that the one extreme, security through the maximization of authority, has its earnest advocates and its equally earnest practitioners. The absolute monarchy of Hobbes has a long history in theory and in action under the benevolent despot exercising the divine right of kings and the naked violence of the ancient or modern tyrant. The libertarian philosopher (who thinks of himself as Hobbes' antithesis) concedes the absolutism of the State under certain conditions or with reference to certain classes of citizen (such as the criminally insane). So does the libertarian politician: we shudder with horror when Sophocles' Creon, condemning Antigone to death, says, "Whomsoever the city may appoint, that man must be obeyed, in little things and great, in just things and unjust. . . . Disobedience is the worst of evils. This it is that ruins cities"; but we accord our approbation to America's Lyndon Johnson when he summons his countrymen to an all-out war on crime and says, "Public order is the first business of Government. When public order breaks down . . . when contempt and mistrust too often characterize public attitudes toward lawful authority, all . . . suffer the consequences. Lawlessness is like a plague."

We suppose that no responsible member of society would argue that only individual liberty exists, with no sovereignty whatever inhering in The State. Nor has any society ever *evolved* on that principle. The record of social enterprise is strewn with the wreckage of the "intentional communities" (or as they are significantly known, even to themselves, utopias) established on the basis of absolute liberty of their adult members and entered into not by accident of birth, but by personal choice. Some such communities have endured a few months, some a few years, a very few some very few decades; all of them within the boundaries of the ordinary State, under its laws, and at more or less continual odds with it; but all of them composed of like-minded individuals of a character and purpose so radically different from the generality of their time and place that no lesson could be drawn even from their successful operation and their capacity (which none of them has ever displayed) to endure much beyond the lives of their founders.

It would seem, then, that the libertarian extreme, in contrast with the totalitarian, is without example in theory or history and insusceptible of dialectical confrontation except as a straw man. But its very nonexistence is an argument that The State is by nature totalitarian—that it is *and must be*. The assertion of individual liberty as absolute (be it only to take a Saturday night bath) is nothing more or less than the assertion that an omelette can be made without breaking eggs. We hear that men are not eggs and are not to be broken; but the point is unaffected. Define liberty as nothing more than deviation from the norm; let the deviation, as to compulsory vaccination, compulsory public schooling, or compulsory military service, spread unchecked and you find the house divided against itself, and falling. Deviation extrapolated is random behavior; in society, chaos.

In mechanics the second law of thermodynamics denies equilibrium to a dynamically balanced tension; without external energy input (i.e., authority, in our argument) the maximization of entropy (or disorder, or, in our argument, liberty) is unexceptionable in dynamic systems and the unexceptionable end is disintegration. So, too, the condition of a biological organism's survival is the coordination of its parts, and their incoordinate behavior fatal. The analogy of politics with mechanics and biology is dangerous, but who, on the face of the matter, would quarrel with Plato's contention that the best unified State, with each man in his proper place, doing his proper work, is the most just, that there can be "no greater evil than discord and distraction and plurality where unity ought to reign, or any greater good than the bond of unity"?

The opposite threat of the random is, of course, the rigid. Opposite, yes—but equal? Given that the community is indispensable to the very survival of the social animal, and his survival the first condition of his having any liberty at all, is it not easier contended (indeed, self-evident) that the community's (and therefore its members') chance of survival is better under totalitarianism than it is under that unrestrained liberty which goes by the name of anarchy; and to opt, when opt we must, for the former as, at least, the lesser evil? If our reasoning is agreeable to this point, does it not follow that the insistence that any liberty whatever beyond the reach of the law is the sanction of "the ruin of cities"? The straw pours forth from a thousand wounds in our straw man, and our argument proves to be the absurdum our auditors suspected from the first. But not quite.

We have to dispose of him (should such a *rara* be found) who dares to maintain that there are liberties protected by reason from The State power (and therefore to be protected by statute) on one of two grounds: *Either* they do not threaten the existence of The State (but where shall we find such liberties, if my Saturday night bath is excluded?) *or* they are so proper to human life that it is not worth living without them (as those latter-day Patrick Henrys seem to be saying when they cry, "Better dead than Red") and the proper justification for The State's existence, its service to man, is lost with their suppression. And there are such men; not merely patriotic orators or religious or irreligious fanatics, but men of comparable intellectual weight to Hobbes and his autocracy. At least there would seem to be, and if they will now step forward the issue may yet be joined.

Who will come to the support of the humane farmer who sheltered the runaway slave—or, in the same era, and on the same issue, that John Brown who took up arms and attacked the United States of America, and was hanged for it, and of whom millions of men defending that same United States of America were singing a few years later, "His soul goes marching on"? Who speaks for liberty untouchable by authority, let the laws, yes, and The State itself, fall where they will?

Why, the Founding Fathers themselves—on the first Fourth of July, appending their signatures to the document that was, and still is, heard 'round the world'. The words were written by Jefferson in collaboration with Adams and Franklin, proclaiming that all men, created equal, are endowed by their Creator with certain inalienable rights. "Inalienable," in one authoritative dictionary, means "not transferable; that cannot rightfully be taken away." The State cannot touch them rightfully, but only wrongfully. And if it touches them wrongfully? The Founders would not allow it to touch them at all: "Congress shall make no law abridging . . ."

Another dictionary of the highest repute defines "inalienable" as "incapable of being alienated, surrendered, or transferred to another," and explicates: "That is inalienable which one cannot give away or dispose of even if one wishes." These rights are more than inherent (Jefferson's first draft of the Declaration referred to them as "inherent and inalienable"); they cannot be got rid of. They are more properly mine than my possessions or my person; they are more properly mine than my life, which I can give up, if I wish, to my family, my friend, or my country. *I cannot surrender my rights if I want to.*

Let us look at the matter in such a way that the professors of fine print cannot fudge it: Does "inalienable" mean "inalienable" or doesn't it? And if it does, does The State fall as the man stands, or doesn't it? This, and nothing else, is the issue here, and Jefferson's is as good a way as any other of encapsulating it. Or is the Declaration to be dismissed as so much Fourth of July euphoria?

Along with the contemporaneous Virginia Bill of Rights (which used the term "inherent," and which held that as men cannot divest themselves of their rights, neither can they "by any compact deprive or divest their posterity"), the Declaration, in proclaiming inalienability, seems to make a modest innovation on the doctrine of Locke (to whom Jefferson acknowledged the Founders' obvious indebtedness). Locke held, indeed, that "freedom from absolute, arbitrary power is so necessary to, and closely joined with, a man's preservation, that he cannot part with it but by what forfeits his preservation and life together." No man, then, has a right to give or sell himself into *absolute* slavery, according to Locke, for a man, having no power over his own life, has no power to give another that power; but "having by his fault forfeited his own life by some act that deserves death, he to whom he has forfeited it may, when he has him in his power, delay to take it, and make use of him to his own service; and he does him no injury by it. For whenever he finds the hardship of his slavery to outweigh the value of his life, it is in his power, by resisting the will of his master, to draw on himself the death he desires. . . ."

However irresistible Locke's delineation, there is something wistful in the logic that guarantees liberty to the slave by granting him the right to bring his own death upon himself at the hands of his master; if this isn't suicide (which Locke forbids) it avoids it by an intolerable technicality. To be sure, Locke's deprivation of liberty rested upon wrong-doing of a capital character in which the wrong-doer has forfeited his life, and the American Founders forbade neither imprisonment nor capital punishment of duly convicted criminals. But slavery is something else—involuntary servitude, without wrong-doing, without conviction, and without even the color of merited punishment.

The great contradiction in theory between liberty and authority also was the great contradiction in practice on that first Fourth of July. The majority of the Southern signers of the Declaration were owners of slaves, including Jefferson (who subsequently freed his) and the author of the Virginia Bill of Rights, George Mason of Virginia (who had five hundred "blacks"). But Jefferson was at least willing to live with the contradiction. The Declaration as he wrote it contained twenty-eight charges against the British Crown. In the course of three days of continuous debate in the Continental Congress (here is a tale told out of school more often than in) the twenty-eighth charge was struck out "in complaisance," Jefferson wrote in his notes, "to South Carolina and Georgia," adding, "Our Northern brethren also I believe felt a little tender under those censures; for tho' their people had very few slaves themselves yet they had been pretty considerable carriers of them to others."

This was the deletion:

"He"—George II—"has waged cruel war against human nature itself, violating its most sacred rights of life and liberty in the persons of a distant people who never offended him, captivating and carrying

47

them into slavery in another hemisphere, or to incur miserable death in their transportation thither. This piratical warfare, the opprobrium of *infidel* powers, is the warfare of the *Christian* king of Great Britain. Determined to keep open market where MEN should be bought and sold, he has prostituted his negative for suppressing every legislative attempt to prohibit or restrain this execrable commerce. . . ."

Trapped by the dilemma, like all the philosophers and politicians and apostles before him and since; trapped like the Ohio farmer who might have written the twenty-eighth charge (had his humaneness not overcome him) and still obeyed the law that mocked the charge; Thomas Jefferson knew, as did everyone else, that the slave trade, in which the English engaged, depended upon slavery itself, in which the English did not engage, while their American colonists did. He knew that "our Northern brethren" were hot competitors of the English slave-traders. He knew that a "market where MEN [are] bought and sold" was carried on, not by George III, but by Philadelphians around the corner (so to say) from Independence Hall.

The British Cabinet called the Declaration "frivolous," and a slave state governor of later time explained that "our forefathers, when they proclaimed this truth to be self-evident, were not in the best mood to become philosophers . . . They were much excited." A slavery preacher called "every word of it . . . the liberty and equality claimed by infidelity." And John C. Calhoun maintained to the end that "it is a great and dangerous error to suppose that all people are equally entitled to liberty." That all men are created equal had been asserted—and in those words by Aquinas in the Thirteenth Century—again and again throughout history. That *as men* they had certain rights, inherent, inalienable rights that no government might ever invade was palpable nonsense in the world of hard-headed realism. But that "nonsense" was the real revolution made by men who created a form of government that astonished the world, and a system of government that still astonishes it.

Between 1861 and 1865 the American people paid a terrible price for the contradiction between the theoretical "nonsense" and the practical problem posed by its application. They are still paying it, in Harlem and Watts, Detroit and Newark, in Arkansas, Mississippi, Alabama, and Chicago. The scales are tipped from day to day, now this way, now that, men crying, on the one side, "Law and order," and on the other, "Freedom *now.*" There is not much theorizing. Each sets his own limit of liberty—or authority—in the heat of the moment. When The State power grows in the direction of liberty, it grows at the expense of the liberty of the individual states within the Union, or of the restaurateur who cherishes the liberty to serve whom he will; when it grows in the direction of authority, it provides no compensating liberty, as in the Supreme Court's *Ginzburg* decision of 1967, when a publisher found himself in prison because the advertising for a book he published (not the book itself) was salaciously "titillating"—a nice point, as the lawyers call it, for Nine Old Men.

But, while the line wavered from case to case, the oldest of the Nine Old Men of our time stood pat for liberty unlimited—almost. "In the history of the Supreme Court there has been no more zealous, no more single-minded advocate of individual liberty than Justice Black"; the assessment, by the *New York Times,* is not widely challenged. Hugo Lafayette Black believes, he says, that "there *are* 'absolutes' in our Bill of Rights,

49

and they were put there on purpose by men who knew what words meant, and meant their prohibitions to be 'absolutes'. . . . I understand that it is rather old-fashioned and shows a slight naivete to say that 'no law' means no law, but what it says is, 'Congress shall make no law.' "[8]

This is plain, and lonely, speaking. It rejects the balancing of freedom and security, even to the point of passionate dissent from the conviction of Communist leaders for conspiring to advocate the overthrow of the government. It excludes libel and slander, even obscenity, from punishment; and Justice Black has said so, and has held so. No American may be made to answer for his speech, his writing, his belief, or his association. At eighty-three the senior member of the Court was as peppery as ever. A few years earlier his late colleague and close friend, Justice Frankfurter, in a majority opinion made a passing reference to "the so-called Bill of Rights," and Hugo Black's voice rang with something like rage when, in reading his dissent, he said, "This case concerns the Bill of Rights, not the so-called Bill of Rights."

His most eminent supporter was a non-lawyer, a distinguished educator, and his senior by many years, Alexander Meiklejohn, one-time President of Amherst College who died a few years ago at ninety-two. "The First Amendment," said Meiklejohn, "seems to me to be a very uncompromising statement. It admits no exceptions. It tells us that the Congress, and by implica-

---

[8]*Cf.* The French *Declaration of the Rights of Man and of the Citizen* (1789), Article XI of which reads, "The unrestrained communication of thoughts and opinions being one of the most precious Rights of Man, every citizen may speak, write, and publish freely, provided he is responsible for the abuse of this liberty in cases determined by law."

tion, all other agencies of the government are denied any authority whatever to limit the political freedom of the citizens of the United States . . . [It] might have been written, not as it is, but as the Courts of the United States have re-written it in the war-maddened years since 1919. The Amendment might have said, 'Except in times and situations involving Clear and Present Danger to the national security, Congress shall make no law abridging Freedom of Speech.' Or it might have read, 'Only when, in the judgment of the Legislature, the interests of order and security render such action advisable shall Congress abridge the Freedom on Speech.' But the writers of the Amendment did not adopt these phrasings or anything like them . . ."

Meiklejohn hammered the argument home: Individual liberty is not derived from The State or from any of its organs—or from society. It is not bestowed or conferred. It is not revocable by any man or institution under any conditions. It is inherent and inalienable, and it cannot be touched in the name of security. Meiklejohn pointed out again and again that "a general legislative power to act for the security and welfare of the nation was denied by the Constitutional Convention on the ground that it would destroy the basic postulate of popular Self-Government on which the Constitution rests." It is the *Preamble* of the Constitution that contains the celebrated "general welfare" clause, and the Preamble is written in the name, not of Congress or the Government, but of "We, the people." "We Americans have, together, decided to be politically free."

But the great "absolutists" are not *absolute* absolutists. When Meiklejohn says that "the experimental faith by which we Americans have undertaken to live is that suppression is always foolish, freedom is always wise,"

51

he, no more than Hugo Black, allows action a free rein. But the *advocacy* of action against The State *is* protected by the Bill of Rights "where it falls short of incitement," as the late Justice Brandeis said in the *Whitney* case, "and there is nothing to indicate that the advocacy would be immediately acted upon." "Tendency" to incite is not enough; The State has the burden of proving that immediate action would in all probability follow.[9]

There are exceptions, then, in the doctrine of the absolutists of liberty. Justice Black, though he quarrels with the ambiguity of the doctrine, would agree with

---

[9]The *proof* that action would *in all probability* follow speech turns, of course, on the state of mind of the judge and/or jury before which the case is tried. Given the necessary imprecision of the matter, the court's state of mind might well be responsive to strong sentiments held in high places. ". . . On the question of where does free speech move toward public disturbance, my answer would be 'pretty soon' . . . I'd call something a riot sooner than maybe other people might. Don't you think that's the attitude generally of this Nixon Administration?"—Assistant U.S. Attorney General Will Wilson (1969).

In 1969 the "criminal syndicalism" statutes of the Red scare that followed the First World War were still on the books of many states, among them California, which appealed to the U.S. Supreme Court for a ruling which would enable it to proceed against the Black Panthers, in whose newspaper there appeared this advertisement: WANTED DEAD FOR MURDER—S.F. [San Francisco] PIG [policeman] MICHAEL O'BRIEN, followed by O'Brien's home address. (California submitted, among other items, an alleged Panther explosives manual: "Now, to make an actual grenade, a weapon that kills, the following can be done . . ."). Like the federal Smith Act after the Second World War, the criminal syndicalist statutes forbade the teaching or advocacy of violent overthrow, but in the Dennis (1951) and Yates (1957) cases the Supreme Court, bitterly divided, as usual, limited the applicability of the Act to occasions "when the group is of sufficient size and cohesiveness, is sufficiently oriented towards action, and other circumstances are such as reasonably to justify apprehension that action will occur." The "apprehension," as well as the determination of size, cohesiveness, orientation, and "other circumstances," is, of course, The State's; and in any subsequent adjudication, a defense would have to be attempted against the justifiability of the apprehension of The State's expert representatives on the scene at the time—and against their determination of size, cohesion, orientation, and "other circumstances."

Holmes that "the First Amendment, while prohibiting legislation against free speech as such, cannot have been, and obviously was not, intended to give immunity to every form of language." I am not free, in Holmes' classic expression, falsely to cry fire in a crowded theatre—or to counsel murder, or to hand a small child what I know is a strychnine pill and tell him that it is candy. To say that speech may be controlled, to say that I may not sing at the top of my voice outside my neighbor's open window in the middle of the night, is not the same thing as to say that speech may be forbidden.

"There *are* absolutes in our Bill of Rights." *Hélas!*— other times, other opinions. As mass public protests grew in the United States at the end of the 1960s, the decisions of the liberal "Warren Court," prior to the retirement of the Chief Justice, swung more and more frequently to a new 5-to-4 alignment, with the decisive vote for the limitation of rights cast by Justice Black. Writing the majority opinion in *Adderly vs. Florida,* Black upheld the arrests of Negro demonstrators who were standing peaceably on public property in Tallahassee. Said the respected Tom Wicker in the *New York Times,* "If that is not allowed, what is? Justice Black's views would appear to a layman to prohibit all but the most pallid means of public protest." The venerable jurist sharply distinguished speech, writing, and assembly from "conduct," although the Court had previously held that the burning of draft cards was "symbolic speech." In a celebrated television interview, he elaborated: "I've never said that freedom of speech gives people the right to tramp up and down the streets by the thousands, either saying things that threaten others, with real literal language, or that threatened them because of the circumstances under which they do it . . . [The First Amendment] doesn't have anything that protects a man's right to walk around and around and around my house, if he wants to, fasten my family up into the house, make them afraid to go out of doors." "It is not true," he added, "that the only way to protest anything is to go out and do it in the streets," and he cited elections, church gatherings, and meetings as acceptable means of protest and dissent. "But," said Wicker, "if Southern Negroes had restricted themselves to those means, rather than resorting to boycotts, demonstrations, marches, and sit-ins, even such meager gains as they have made would have been a long time—if ever—in coming."

When we look for the absolute antithesis to absolute autocracy, we nowhere find it in jurisprudence. To permit The State to move against my liberty is to circumscribe my liberty, whether I am "controlled" or "forbidden." To permit it to do so in the name of national security is to circumscribe my liberty. To permit it to do so because I am injuring or have injured another—though no one would defend the contrary position—is to circumscribe my liberty, and to permit it to do so because I am thought to be injuring another, or because I might injure another, is to circumscribe my liberty still further—my liberty, that is, to do as I please. My liberty to walk down Main Street nude is circumscribed as disorderly conduct. *At some point* I belong to The State—as I discovered when Officer Sweeney would not let me run my bath.

And in one of the most disconsoling cases ever brought to the bar in America, the authority of The State to seize a citizen who had not been charged with a crime, strip him of his property, deport him without

54

a hearing, and imprison him indefinitely, was upheld by the United States Supreme Court in an opinion written by none other than "that single-minded advocate of individual liberty," Justice Black. Korematsu was an American of Japanese descent, one of 112,000 rounded up and, on two-weeks notice, shipped from the West Coast to abandoned stables (one family to a stall) in the interior of the country, in April of 1942, on order of the Western Command of the Army of the United States. Although the Commanding General, in his official report of the action, referred to all of them as "subversive," as belonging to "an enemy race" whose "racial strains are undiluted," and as constituting "over 112,000 potential enemies at large," not one of the 112,000 was then, or ever thereafter, accused of an act of disloyalty. But Justice Black held, for the majority, that "we cannot reject as unfounded the judgment of the military authorities and of Congress that there were disloyal members of that population, whose number and strength could not be precisely and quickly ascertained . . . We uphold the exclusion order as of the time it was made . . . Korematsu was not excluded from the Military Area because of hostility to him or his race. He *was* excluded because we are at war with the Japanese Empire, because the properly constituted military authorities feared an invasion of our West Coast and felt constrained to take proper security measures, because they decided that the military urgency of the situation demanded that all citizens of Japanese ancestry be segregated from the West Coast temporarily, and, finally, because Congress, reposing its confidence in this time of war in our military leaders—as inevitably it must—determined that they should have the power to do this . . ."

The Korematsu decision evoked some of the most furious dissents ever heard from the highest bench. Justice Roberts condemned the conviction of a citizen "as a punishment for not submitting to imprisonment in a concentration camp"—Korematsu had not reported for deportation—"solely because of his ancestry." Justice Murphy, pointing out that martial law had not been declared, called the decision a "legalization of racism" and a denial that "under our system of law individual guilt is the sole basis of deprivation of rights." And Justice Jackson acidly protested that Korematsu's crime "consists merely of being present in the state whereof he is a citizen, near the place where he was born, and where all his life he has lived"; Korematsu was a criminal because "he belonged to a race from which there is no way to resign."

"I believe," said Justice Black, ten or fifteen years after Korematsu, and in connection with another case entirely, "that it is time enough for government to step in to regulate people when they do something, not when they say something." This is the same Justice Black who wrote the Court's opinion that Korematsu was properly "regulated" not for something he did, not for something he said, but for being where he had always been. Korematsu's "absolute freedom" was struck down as handily as mine to sit in my rocker strumming my electric guitar the night that Officer Sweeney rapped at my door. "Nothing," said Chief Justice Vinson in the celebrated *Dennis* case, "is more certain in modern society than the principle that there are no absolutes." Either Black is dead wrong—and was wrong by his own lights in Korematsu—or Vinson is wrong. And until we know which, how are we to establish a society whose first principle is liberty?

CHAPTER
V

The Criminality of Conscience

From Antigone through Martin Luther to Martin Luther King the issue of liberty has turned on the existence of a higher law than that of The State. When the authors of the American Declaration of Independence bottomed their case on "the laws of nature and of nature's God," they were not being prolix. They were Deists who found the limitation of governmental power in divine revelation; but they were also political philosophers who harked back to the *ius naturale* of Roman jurisprudence which derived from pagan as well as religious sources among the Chinese, the Hebrews, and the Greeks. The natural law doctrine is in limbo nowadays, maintained largely (if not exclusively) by Catholic philosophers against the modern materialist position that, as all political power emanates from man, so all human law is made by man fully enfranchised in a fully representative government.[10]

---

[10]The "modern" position isn't all that modern. An historical (and historic) instance of it is the revolutionary French *Declaration of the Rights of Man and of the Citizen* of 1789, which asserts that "the nation is essentially the source of all sovereignty; nor can any INDIVIDUAL, or ANY BODY OF MEN, be entitled to any authority which is not expressly derived from it." Nor is constitutional confusion in the matter modern: The article preceding this one in the French *Declaration* asserts that "the end of all political associations is the preservation of *the natural and imprescriptible rights of man.*" [Italics mine] Rights are, apparently, natural to man—*and* derived from The State.

Natural law—if it exists—is not made by man, but discovered by him in his own nature: thus, and only thus, are his rights indeed inalienable. They are not, said Alexander Hamilton, "to be rummaged for among old parchments or musty records. They are written as with a sunbeam, in the whole volume of human nature, by the hand of divinity itself and can never be erased or obscured by mortal power." To be a man is to possess those "sacred rights," antecedent to and superior to the *ius civile* which stands or falls by virtue of its conformity to the *ius naturale*. Cicero asserted that a statute contravening the natural law is no statute at all, any more than "the regulations of a band of robbers."

But a thoroughly secular society in a secular age is not to be governed by the "hand of divinity itself;" nor is a pragmatic society in a pragmatic age likely to look for sacred rights in a sunbeam. Most modern jurists dismiss the concept of natural law—and Jefferson and Hamilton with it—as superstition or, perhaps, fideism disguised as philosophy.

But those who still maintain the doctrine, and who maintain that it is confirmed by what Darwin called "the natural light of reason," without regard to faith, argue that there is no defense of liberty against The State unless men are under a law which is higher than The State's. The only answer to the absolutist State is an absolute standard by which human law is tested, a Constitution which measures all constitutions. Failing such objective standard, there is no way to justify noncompliance with a bad law or resistance to a bad State. The "naturalists" point to the indictment of the Nazi leaders at Nuremberg which charged them with "crimes against humanity." Their alleged offenses were legal under German law, illegal only if there were a law transcending those of the sovereign German State and making universally criminal those acts which offended human nature itself.

Law, including natural law, would seem to require a lawmaker or lawgiver. In Judeo-Christian doctrine this is God, Who stamps His ineradicable plan—Eternal Law—upon the soul of his human creatures. This stamp is the natural law. Man is given reason with which to discern it and free will with which to follow it in the pursuit of a destiny beyond this life and, therefore, beyond The State. It is the business of The State to "secure," i.e., make secure, the natural rights man has from God; thus far, and no further, may organized society go. Christian doctrine on the issue was enunciated in the Thirteenth Century by St. Thomas Aquinas: "Human law does not bind a man in conscience . . . [and if it conflicts with man's participation in the Eternal Law] human laws should not be obeyed."

In the realm of faith the natural law is in part explicated, in part indicated, in the commandments of God in Holy Writ. But how are we to understand the commandments of God, including, for hard example, "Thou shalt not kill," when God Himself has commanded to kill? Does "kill" mean what we call murder, and not war? And if murder, is it murder for a husband to kill his wife's lover under the "unwritten law," or for the Nazis, under the law of their own country, to exterminate the Jews?

The Church arrogates to itself the interpretation of God's commandments, but the history of the Church is the history of schism and war between churchmen and churches over irreconcilable interpretations. Some denominations accept war as the will of God, and some as the ineluctable consequence of the Pauline doctrine that "the powers that be are ordained of God;" others maintain that the "just war" alone warrants The State's conscription of its citizens to kill. (But who is to determine that *this* war is just, and who is to tell the members of the denomination who find themselves on the "unjust" side that they are to refuse to fight on the pain of death for desertion or treason?) Still others, the historic "peace churches," like the primitive Christendom of the First Century reject war altogether and advise their communicants to do likewise. In the War of 1812 the American Shakers, who had been mobbed, reviled, and imprisoned by their countrymen during the Revolution, procalimed that "God has required of us to abstain from all acts of violence against the lives of our fellow creatures." It followed that they had to obey this requirement "even at the expense of our lives," their duty to God being "paramount over all other duties." (By the time of the Civil War, President Lincoln granted them military exemption.)

The concept of the *person*—the human individual—was transmitted from Greek Stoicism to Christian theology through Hellenistic Judaism and Roman jurisprudence. As an individual, man may be required to surrender his goods and services to meet the needs of his fellow men and the human community; but not to the point that jeopardizes his (or another's) person. His person is more than his life, but his life is sacred as the vessel (here below, at least) of his person. So is his liberty. His person may not be used as a means to any end whatever; it may not be sacrificed to the common good; it may not be discarded (or eliminated) as useless. His person is his own under God; unanswerable to any man or aggregation of men. It has individual duties to itself and others; it may be appealed to, reasoned with, prayed for, persuaded; but it may not be compelled. To require a man to kill another—for whatever reason—is as much a violation of the *persona* as to require him to kill himself.

The despised Shakers were few, like those of the other "peace churches," Quakers, Mennonites, Brethren, Jehovah's Witnesses, and (as regards actual combat) Seventh Day Adventists. Their exemption from war constituted, as it still constitutes, no "clear and present danger" to their country. *But what if they should be many?* In that case, with a million or ten million men refusing to fight, the few countries that now exempt conscientious objectors from military service would indeed be confronted with a clear and present danger; and on the doctrine those countries themselves have recognized, they would have to accept what no sovereign society has ever yet accepted, the probability, if not the certainty, of their own uncontested destruction. The fact that the United States Congress grants such exemption as a "privilege," not as a "right," would be a legal sanction for the withdrawal of the privilege. But the *fact* that the Shakers and their kind would not fight would be unaffected. I discussed this point twenty-five years ago with a man much interested in it, the son (if I recall correctly) of a Mennonite mother. "That," said General (then Lieutenant Colonel) Lewis B. Hershey, Director of Selective Service, "would be a hard one, for this or any other country. I can't imagine a solution to it."

I can: should the number of war resisters ever reach the point where the country's military security appeared to be in danger, the liberty would fall (as mine fell before Officer Sweeney's nightstick) and the absolute power of The State, even the best of States, would

61

emerge from the shadows in which it dozes peacefully under ordinary conditions. Article XIII, Section 1, of the United States Constitution forbids involuntary servitude except as a punishment for crime, but conscription for military *or* civilian service (such as fire-fighting at the command of Officer Sweeney) is, whatever else it may be, involuntary servitude. The courts of the United States (and of all other countries) have never let Article XIII, Section 1, stand in the way of conscription. How could they—and still perform their Constitutional duty of providing for "the common defense"?

When the churches disagree (as they always have) as to what is Caesar's, or I disagree with one or all of them, my only guide is my conscience. The otherwise law-abiding man, when he breaks the law, pleads the necessity of conscience and always has; the term is as often as not used for the command of God or the voice within us with which that command is issued. "The rights of conscience," says Jefferson in his *Notes on the State of Virginia*, "we never submitted, we could not submit [to government]. We are answerable for them to our God." We have only, then, to discover what conscience is, and what it compels, and our troubles are over; we have discovered the limit of The State's power and, so, the scope of individual liberty. The discovery has not been made, nor does it seem likely that it will be.[11] For my conscience tells me X and yours

---

[11]The volubility of statesmen on the sovereignty of conscience has generally failed them when they got down to the business of writing State papers (including constitutions). A cursory survey yields only two outright affirmations in public documents—both of them in the context of denominational liberty in religion. In 1647 the *Agreement of the People of England,* presented by the Levellers to the Army Council, and by the Council to the Commons, asserted that, in matters of religion, "we cannot remit a tittle of what our consciences dictate to be the mind of God without wilful sin;" and the

tells you not—X, and The State's only hope of allowing me the liberty of what I call conscience is its undependable decision that I appear to be, and generally have been, a "conscientious" man. And it is The State—equipped with no true instrument for the purpose—that will do the deciding. How can it help but overrule my claim to acquittal on the ground that it was my conscience that compelled me to blow up the Brooklyn Bridge?

The lawyers talk of "an order of values" in the claim of conscience; but if conscience is beyond the reach of The State, how can The State or its lawyers, or its laws, presume to discriminate among acts of conscience? As a Mormon, I am constrained in conscience to advocate polygamy; as a Jehovah's Witness, I am constrained to play anti-Catholic phonograph records over a loudspeaker in a street whose residents are 90% Catholic; as an atheist, I am constrained in conscience to refuse to pledge my allegiance to the American flag "under God"; as a churchman I am constrained to refuse to swear an oath of loyalty to The State. In the courts the law upholds my right of conscience in every one of these acts; I am told that The State cannot touch me, even though I offend others and even assault public morality or (in wartime, when I refuse to pledge allegiance) sow dissent in a beleaguered community. How, then, can it touch me when my conscience requires me to discard

---

°

Virginia Bill of Rights (preceding the Declaration of Independence by three weeks) found all men "equally entitled to the free exercise of religion, according to the dictates of conscience." Confronted with the claim of conscience, the United States Supreme Court said that "the Bill of Rights recognized that in the domain of conscience there is a moral power higher than the State;" confronted with the same claim in another case, it said that "civil government cannot let any group ride roughshod over others simply because their 'consciences' tell them to do so."

my clothing in public or, indeed, to blow up a bridge? How can *it* determine "an order of values;" how can *it* decide what conscience is and still leave conscience free?

It can't. So it does what it can't do either: it decides what conscience is, and in its own worldly terms it would be derelict (as no State ever has been) if it didn't. It decides, in the case before it, by submitting me to its investigation and interrogation, as if conscience were susceptible (as Philosopher Sidney Hook says it is) of "rational analysis" (by, of course, The State, which is assumed to be the competent custodian of rationality). What, then, had become of Jefferson's insistence that we are answerable to God alone, and not to government, for our rights of conscience? What has become of Aquinas in the Thirteenth Century, or of Chief Justice Hughes in the Twentieth?—"The essence of religion is a belief in a relation to a God involving duties superior to those arising from any human relation." What has become of the Supreme Court's classic finding in *Girouard* that "throughout the ages, men have suffered death rather than subordinate their allegiance to God to the authority of The State. Freedom of religion guaranteed by the First Amendment is the product of that struggle!"? What has become of my "most fundamental personal values," on whose basis the Solicitor General of the United States, a former dean of the Harvard Law School, validates my *moral,* if not my *legal,* right to disobey? The State, when I ask it these questions, shakes its head sadly. God is not dead; he's alive and well in the Department of Justice.

I sympathize with The State in its dilemma, but I cannot help it. I dare not help it without putting all liberty on the block. Today my conscience compels me to spit on the sidewalk; The State (though my sputum is uninfected) arrests me on its "clear and present danger" doctrine and calls my claim to conscience self-evidently false. I yield my conscience to The State—and tomorrow it arrests me for refusing to pay my war tax. In yielding today, in the matter of expectoration, I have yielded the principle that would alone protect liberty tomorrow.

I say I sympathize with The State. The good State—such as mine—writhes in its agony to protect my liberty and assures me, in earnestness, on its highest judicial authority, that the "working principle" that "finally emerges from 'clear and present danger' cases" is that the substantive evil must be *extremely serious* and the degree of imminence *extremely high* before utterances can be punished." It writhes—but I cannot acquiesce in a doctrine so arrant and so deadly. The State that is permitted to determine the extreme has been permitted to determine the mean. I have let it become the arbiter of conscience—liberty's only security against it.

If conscience resists definition in many respects, it has general acceptance in at least one: It is not a people's or a majority's, but a man's; one man's. *My* conscience is not, and cannot be, the property of a pastor, a premier, or a parliament. It is no more the property of the whole community together than it is a majority's. It reprobates democracy as readily as it does tyranny. Though it may listen more sympathetically to the former than to the latter, it answers them both with identical assumption: "Men of Athens"—or, "Man of Athens," it matters not which—"I love and honor you, but—" What his conscience demands of the conscientious individual, this he does. And at that moment he is an anarchist, as much so as the Muslim who faces west to pray

65

when the rest all face east, or the American who blows up the bridge or sets forth with his gun to liberate the slaves in Bloody Kansas (or runs the bath-water when the mayor has forbidden it under martial law). There is exactly as much political theory in the tea spilled in Boston Harbor as there is in the blood spilled at Lexington and Concord.

Whoever breaks the law for whatever reason—call it what he will—is a common criminal, however uncommon a man with however uncommon a motivation. What jurisprudence calls equity may suspend the sentence of the starving man who filched a loaf of bread, or of the Jehovah's Witness who would not let his dying child have a blood transfusion; legend may acquit Robin Hood for the use he made of the money he stole; and history may acquit Gandhi for having taken salt from the sea without paying the British salt tax—but they are criminals all, along with every first and last signer of the Declaration of Independence—lawbreakers "laying the axe to the root of all established government." In equity we try to distinguish between the conscientious and the unconscionable criminal. If he transgresses openly, and not furtively, and freely accepts the consequences of his crime and "turns himself in" to pay the penalty, he seems to be conscientious; thus Gandhi, pleading guilty of "evading" the salt tax, asked for "the highest penalty that can be inflicted upon me for what in law is a deliberate crime and what appears to me to be the highest duty of a citizen." But John Brown is thought to have been conscientious, too, and he neither surrendered himself nor invited the penalty he paid. So, too, he who means to commit the crime in the interest of others and not in his own, or (though he, too, may be a beneficiary) means to attack a social injustice, seems to be conscientious; but it may be that the conscientious or unconscionable Negro who refuses to move to the back of the bus may in fact mean neither; and it is possible, even probable, that some of the white and black militants "liberating" university buildings on behalf of Negro rights are not as much interested in Negro rights as they are in promoting what is sometimes called a rumble. Men's motives are marvelously mixed, and just as marvelously inaccessible to definitive determination by courts of law; and in any case they are peripheral to the problem here.

The problem here is the individual's obedience and disobedience to The State in the person of its laws, not the purity of his motivation or the consequences of his act. He says he means to change a bad law and has no other objective. He is wrong, though his course of action may (like that of Martin Luther King or the rioters of the ghetto or the campus) actually have that effect. There is only one way for a citizen to change the law and that way is prescribed by his country's Constitution. The claimant of conscience, even though he hopes to change the law by defying it, is not, as such, a political man performing a political act; a political man changes the law by the rule of law, which provides the means of effecting change. To set about changing the law by breaking it—if this be the purpose of civil disobedience—is to perform a political act in a manner impermissible to a political man.[12]

---

[12]Acts of civil disobedience are, however, not uncommonly performed for the purpose of testing the validity of a statute. Under these circumstances the nonpolitical act has a clearly political character. There is no way for a citizen to challenge the constitutionality of a law except by breaking it. This paradoxical procedure is not only recognized by the juridical process; it is actually encouraged. In acquitting a member of the German-American Bund who, just prior to Pearl Harbor, counseled refusal of military service

67

There are two immediate difficulties here, both of them suggestive that The State in fact brooks no claim whatever to a "higher law." The first is the *insignificance* of conscience *vis à vis* The State: What is a conscience for, and how can the "rights of conscience" be argued, if the superior right of The State is acknowledged to slap down a man every time he exercises it? Here is an empty "right," if ever there was one; and all that there is to be said for its practical significance is its expression of God's will to be punished on earth and rewarded in heaven. But in that case it is only on a religious view that conscience has any effective liberty, while here below its liberty exists at the pleasure of The State.

The second difficulty is as troublesome. I am told that the way to change the law is to campaign for its amendment or repeal by a better law—and meanwhile to go on obeying it. I am told by the *Washington Post* that "those who disagree with the policies of the government have available to them a whole arsenal of orderly and lawful devices for changing those policies. Those who dislike an administration in power have a whole assortment of democratic processes by which the administration can be changed. The proper place for opposition is on the forum, the hustings and at the ballot box. The proper means is orderly debate and argument." Good enough, if the obedience required of me does not violate

on the ground that the Selective Service Act unconstitutionally excluded Bund members from "sensitive" posts, the U.S. Supreme Court held that "one with innocent motives, who honestly believes that a law is unconstitutional and, therefore, not obligatory, may well counsel that the law shall not be obeyed; that its command shall be resisted until a court shall have held it valid . . ." Even after a court (including the highest court) has sustained a law, disobedience is an accepted way of challenging it and has reversed innumerable decisions which otherwise would have stood.

my conscience until such time as, by orderly debate and argument, I have persuaded a majority of my country to change the administration or its policies. I can endure a 25-mile-per-hour speed limit until such time as I can get it changed to 30, or a Saturday garbage collection until I can get it changed to Monday. I can endure no end of *prohibitory* laws—all the more lightly if they forbid me things I don't want much to do, such as sell narcotics or shoot my tiresome neighbor. But there are mandatory laws which command me to perform. The runaway slave is at my door in Ohio; a Negro enters my restaurant in Atlanta; the truant officer comes to my home to order me to take my child to the "worldly" school forbidden by my Amish religion.[13] What then? Am I to do the wrong—according to my conscience—and go on doing it until such time as the legislature permits (or commands) me to do right? The State's answer is, and must be, "Yes—or put yourself at war with The State." I may do the required wrong with "mental reservations," with uncomplacent, even tortured, conscience; The State has no way to subdue my reservations and no interest in doing so. The State commands the act: I perform the act: it has got what it wants of me; if it has my compliance, it will survive without my enthusiasm.

Or perhaps I am not required to do, but only to abide (at no inconvenience, except to conscience) the wrong commanded others by The State or, just as likely, un-

[13]In 1967 the United States Supreme Court—by one-man majority—refused to review the conviction of an Amish farmer in Kansas who refused to send his daughter to school on the ground of the Biblical injunction, "Be not conformed to this World." (Rom. 12:2) Because the Amish refuse to litigate, the defense was conducted by the National Committee for Amish Religious Freedom, composed of leaders of other faiths.

forbidden by The State and commanded by convention. I am to stand by, distressed, to be sure, and see the wrong perpetrated and proliferated and raise no overt voice, no overt finger—and thus serve as an accomplice in the wrongdoing of others. In October 1968, nine Roman Catholic Priests, missionaries, and laymen were convicted in Baltimore, Maryland, of burning military conscription files (an act they admitted). In the course of their trial, the prosecutor stated that in the view of the Federal Government a reasonable man could hold the view (as the defendants did) that the American war in Vietnam was illegal; and the Government conceded that the defendants were reasonable men. None of them was eligible for conscription, and they had acted to disengage themselves from complicity in a war they considered illegal—and which The State thought they might reasonably consider so.[14]

If a man cannot confer his conscience upon The State, and The State cannot permit him to do whatever his conscience dictates, the two can abide together only by happy accident, like a Hatfield and a McCoy who do not happen to meet on the street. Fortunately, few men are so sure of the dictates of conscience as to move to bring down The State on this occasion or that. Most come, in sufficient time, to recognize the dictate as

---

[14]"By God," said that reasonable man, Ralph Waldo Emerson, of the Fugitive Slave Law of 1850, "I will not obey this filthy enactment." Other reasonable "anarchists" did not disengage themselves so easily from complicity: "In consequence of helping some 2700 slaves to freedom, Thomas Garrett, Quaker merchant of Wilmington, Delaware, met prosecution after prosecution, fine after fine, that finally reduced his comfortable means to bankruptcy. After the sheriff's sale that took his last asset, a pompous official said that he hoped this would cure him of law breaking. Said Thomas: 'Friend, I haven't a dollar in the world, but if thee knows a fugitive who needs a breakfast, send him to me.' " (J.C. Furnas, *Goodbye to Uncle Tom,* New York, Sloane, 1956. p. 210)

nothing but the still, small voice of private interest; or they hesitate to set one man's dictate (be it even their own) above the contrary dictate of the men of conscience around them and in their government; or they lose heart at the prospect of the unpleasant consequence of heeding the dictate; or they value society, and The State into which it is organized, so highly that, rather than dismember it, they will suffer in conscience yet a while longer or until such time as a more painful violation of it is required. So good men go on living quietly, for one or another of these reasons, in bad states; so, too, men of great goodness remain in office under bad governments they hope to restrain from becoming still worse. Tragic they may be, and tragic their fate, as was that of Baron Ernst von Weizsäcker, who accepted the post of State Secretary of the Nazi Foreign Ministry and was convicted at Nuremberg by his signature on document after document ordering the deportation of Jews to their death, in spite of the uncontradicted testimony of high Allied statesmen and churchmen that he had held on to his dreadful post in the hope (which proved futile) that he might meliorate the Hitler policy by doing so.

So conscience is constrained by the countervailing consideration of its exercise. When the American colonists finally rebelled, they said: "Prudence, indeed, will dictate that governments long established should not be changed for light and transient causes; and accordingly all experience hath shown that mankind are more disposed to suffer, while evils are sufferable, than to right themselves by abolishing the forms to which they are accustomed. But when a long train of abuses and usurptions, pursuing invariably the same object, evinces a design to reduce them under absolute despotism, it is their right, it is their duty, to throw off such government, and to provide new guards for their future security. Such has been the patient suffering of these colonies; and such is now the necessity which constrains them to alter their former systems of government . . ."

The "patient suffering" of the *Declaration* is required by the law, and the "right and duty" forbidden. And the law is right, grounded as it is on the Aristotelian dictum that "no man is a judge in his own cause." You may say that my objectivity is demonstrated by the suffering I bring upon myself as a violater—but how do you know that I have not undertaken the violation for the purpose of exploiting its penalty to my political or economic—or emotional—advantage? How do *I* know that I am not a compulsive sufferer, the victim of a martyr complex? (I have heard Socrates so dismissed.) Am I to sit in judgement on the limit of my own patience, on the length of the train of abuses and usurptions and the clarity with which those abuses and usurptions evince a design to reduce me under absolute despotism? The law as psychologist says No: I am not competent to take it into my own hands in my own case; I have a stake in the outcome.

We are all lawbreakers. When a spectator was killed by deputy sheriffs during the student convulsions in Berkeley, California, in 1969, the ineffable governor of the state said: "He was killed by the first college administrator who said some time ago it was all right to break laws in the name of dissent." But it is not only college administrators—or the founding fathers of the American Republic—who believe in breaking laws. Breathes there a man with soul so subdued that he has never practiced civil disobedience and done his bit for anarchy by violating closing hours or traffic regulations or fireworks

72

ordinances or wartime rationing or the non-transferability of a commutation ticket (or a streetcar transfer)?

The State itself sets the happy-go-lucky example on State occasions. It will not arrest you for obstructing traffic or disorderly conduct or public drunkenness on V-E Day or V-J Day. It will not prosecute you too relentlessly for minor—or, if you're a good Party Man, major—infractions of the municipal building code. It will use its discretionary powers (nowhere delineated in law) to settle an income tax case or forego a criminal prosecution "in the public interest." And it will go further than closing its eye to this celebrant or that miscreant; it will commit civil disobedience in its own right, in the South by resisting racial integration required by the Court, in the North by conducting classroom prayer forbidden by the Court; in a century of peace by denying or abridging the right of citizens to vote on account of color; in a decade of war without the declaration required by the Constitution.

The State's excuses, like ours, are good: "I'm on my way to the hospital, officer. My wife just had a baby boy. Have a cigar." Like us, its needs are unforeseen, its situations suddenly altered. Like us, it is carried away. And like us, The State has a little larceny in its heart and another law in its members. "If," says Shakespeare's Orlando, "I had my liberty, I would do my liking." Give you or me our sovereign liberty—or The State its—and we are conscientious objectors all.

Legislative intent—and often its extent—is unclear, and necessarily so; no law can cover every contingency. Contradictory statutes, and contradictory rulings under the same statute bedevil me. I have got to find my way through the murk, acting uncertainly and finding more leeway in my uncertainty than a man—or a State—can be trusted with. If only I had a standing rule to go by—if only I knew the *ius naturale* with absolute precision and the *ius civile* with equal precision—I should know what moved me to do what. I once met such a man in California, at the time the churches of that state were trying to decide whether to obey a new law requiring them to take a loyalty oath on pain of losing their tax exemption. Meeting him in town one day, I said, "And what are you Jehovah's Witnesses going to do about the loyalty oath?" "Oh," he said brightly, "We swear not at all. Matthew Five, Thirty-four."

Theologians have always cried up lawbreaking in the name of God's dictate to conscience. As Augustine in the Fifth Century: "When God commands a thing to be done against the customs or compact of any people, though it were never by them done heretofore, it is to be done . . . For, as among the powers in man's society the greater authority is obeyed in preference to the lesser, so must God above all;" so the Twentieth Century American hierarch, Eugene Carson Blake, General Secretary of the World Council of Churches: "We must be entirely clear that law is not God. It has always been a basic Christian conviction that there are times when a Christian ought to break the law." When, where, and how a believer should implement Christian doctrine on this point has always been a sticky matter. No end of "Allied" churchmen joined political personages in urging rebellion against the Communist, the Fascist, and especially the Nazi regimes of Europe, and recognized religiously motivated rebels as heroes and martyrs. But these same churchmen, and their heirs, found it more painful to urge lawlessness in their own lands under freer regimes. It was only when the national fabric in the United States was rent with massive dissent from the war in Vietnam that clergymen of all faiths—among them the Protestant Chaplain of Yale University—rose in increasing numbers to the support of young men resisting military service and of fellow-citizens refusing to pay their taxes, or (in violation of the Trading with the Enemy Act, but in obedience to the Scripture, "If thine enemy hunger, feed him.") contributing medical aid to all parts of Vietnam.

Open rebellion on the part of clergymen poses so difficult a problem for the government of a country that considers itself fideistic that their prosecution was notably slow to be undertaken. But in the late 1960's they began to be indicted and convicted under federal law, just as their brethren in the civil rights struggle, white and black, Protestants, Catholics, and Jews, had always been (and continued to be) jailed under the criminal statutes of some of the Southern states. The defendants could quote Holy Writ and the Church Fathers, ancient and modern, in defense of their revolutionary activity, and, of course, the greatest names in their country's political history. "God forbid, we should ever be twenty years without such a rebellion," said Jefferson in 1787. "What country can preserve its liberties, if its rulers are not warned from time to time, that this people preserve the spirit of resistance? Let them take arms . . . What signify a few lives lost in a century or two? . . . The tree of liberty must be refreshed from time to time, with the blood of patriots and tyrants." And Lincoln in his First Inaugural proclaimed "the revolutionary right to dismember or overthrow [the existing government] whenever the people shall grow weary of it," a sacred right "which we hope and believe is to liberate the world."

Let Augustine and Blake assert the primacy of God's

dominion over conscience; no matter. Let Jefferson and Lincoln asseverate the right of violent revolution; no matter. In the 1960's the single practitioners of nonviolent revolution in the name of God were packed off to jail under statutes held constitutional in either the provincial or federal jurisdictions. Among them was Martin Luther King—at whose unrepentent death a year later the President would proclaim a day of national mourning. (The United States Supreme Court found that the Alabama law which King had broken in the name of conscience was untouchable by the United States Constitution. Let Augustine and Blake hold otherwise, and Jefferson and Lincoln; they are not sitting in this court—or in any other.)

CHAPTER
VI

One Obnoxious Man

The political philosophers, like the judges, either disagree flatly with the theologians (and the statesmen they quote) or retreat to crude equivocation or honest ambivalence. "Seditious," "false," "repugnant to civil society," says Hobbes (of course) of the notion "that every man is judge of good and evil actions;" the law "is the public conscience by which he hath already undertaken to be guided." Locke finds it "an inconvenience, I confess, that attends all governments whatsoever, when the governors have brought it to this pass, to be generally suspected of their people ... When [a majority or all of] the people are persuaded in their consciences that their laws, and with them, their estates, liberties, and lives are in danger, and perhaps their religion too, how they will be hindered from resisting illegal force used against them I cannot tell;" a masterpiece of shoulder-shrugging which, in addition, identifies law with liberty and bypasses the issue.

Kant would seem to be foggier still: God is "the power over all" and conscience is "the subjective principle of a responsibility for one's deeds before God;"

plainly "the power over all" is the supreme power commanding loyalty—but we have only to read on a half hundred pages to learn that the supreme power is something else entirely: "Resistance on the part of the people to the supreme legislative power of The State is in no case legitimate; for it is only by submission to the universal legislative will, that a condition of law and order is possible. . . . It is the duty of the people to bear any abuse of the supreme power, even then though it should be considered to be unbearable. And the reason is that any resistance of the highest legislative authority can never but be contrary to the law, and must even be regarded as tending to destroy the whole legal constitution. In order to be entitled to offer such resistance, a public law would be required to permit it. But the supreme legislation would by such a law cease to be supreme, and the people as subjects would be made sovereign over that to which they are subject. . . ."

The philosophers, like the statesmen, do not come to grips with the issue of liberty at all; not as it ordinarily arises in all societies. The liberty of a minority (including a minority of one) is what is at issue, not the liberty of "the people." To speak of "the people" and *their* rights—not of a fraction of them and *its* rights—enables political philosophy to present itself with a manipulable simplification. The collective "people" either reserve or delegate their individual liberties to The State, and The State, by invading them, puts itself at war with the people and (at least in Locke's view, and in Jefferson's and Lincoln's) loses its authority. "The people" then assert or recapture their rights by revolution.

This is the "right of revolution" by Locke's *majority or all*—a revolution which, in a democracy, is possible by ballot and is ordinarily an overthrow of the party in power, not of the form of government or of government itself. This is no insurrection; heads roll, but they roll on their shoulders. Still less is it a confrontation of man with The State, or the anarchy of a majority (or a minority) rejecting the law or the system of law. It is not in the least criminal, any more than was the accession to power of the Nazis in 1933 or the Czechoslovak Communists in 1948; they came to power legally under the parliamentary system of Europe. We may witness the most outrageous devices to pervert the legal process in Berlin or in Prague—or in Jackson, Mississippi—but the color of legitimacy has prevailed. "The people" have judged, by constitutional majority or plurality, and they have judged that "the people's" liberties are safe.

That this judgment is an impious fraud—that the "democratic process" as such does nothing for human liberty—was at last brought home to what the majority of its citizens were pleased to call the land of liberty when the United States was convulsed by its Negro minority at the end of the 1960's. A concatenation of events and processes produced rebellions, proceeding from prayerful nonviolence to "burn, baby, burn," among a people reduced, after three hundred years, to absolute despair of legal redress in a nation which had achieved the summun bonum of King John's Magna Carta: ". . . nor will we condemn him . . . excepting by the legal judgment of his peers, or by the laws of the land." Neither the first ten amendments to the American Constitution, nor the thirteenth, fourteenth, and fifteenth, had provided liberty for the American blacks; and the blacks knew it, and the whites knew it, and the world knew it. White "establishment" spokesmen sonorously proclaimed that "the United States is a society where [the] essential conditions [of liberty] prevail—certain inalienable individual rights are secure, the lawmakers represent the community, the courts and juries are free to interpret the laws without coercion, there are political means available to revise laws that are repressive or unjust."[15] True, true—and black men, weary of crying out against the pretensions that underlay these truths, were at last in the streets exercising Locke's "right of revolution."

Politically the right of revolution is a contradiction in terms. No sovereign State, no "people," writes a Constitution purposively providing for its own dismemberment or dissolution, nor has any philosopher or statesman that I know of suggested that one such be written. Lincoln's assertion of the "revolutionary right" of overthrow—contrasted, in the First Inaugural, with the *"constitutional* right" of amendment—may be supportable, but what appears to be the counter-assertion, in the same address, does not need support: "It is safe to assert that no government proper ever had a provision in its organic law for its own termination." (He was wrong historically, as we shall see later; but the Polish exception was cataclysmic enough to prove the rule.) The United States Constitution is law, the Declaration of Independence is not; and it is the Declaration, not the Constitution that "legalizes" the overthrow of the government. Many of the former colonies, carried away by the July 4 fervor of the Fathers, actually embodied the right of revolution in their Constitutions, either in the preamble or in a Bill of Rights like New Hampshire's, which proclaims that "whenever the ends of

---

[15]*New York Times* editorial, May 7, 1967.

government are perverted . . . the people may, and of right ought to, reform the old, or establish a new government. The doctrine of non-resistance against arbitrary power and oppression is absurd, slavish, and destructive of the good and happiness of mankind." But neither New Hampshire nor any other right-of-revolution state has yet turned a lawbreaker loose.

A nice distinction may be made in terms of the objective of illegal action: Is its intent the overthrow of the existing government in the name of revolution? Or of government (i.e., The State as distinguished from society) itself in the name of anarchy? Or of a single "unjust" law (or set of laws such as those that protected slavery)? This last, too, may come to revolution, though it is usually denominated insurrection, up to the point where it involves the whole society. The principle we are closest concerned with here bridges the distinction: Who breaks *any* law, with *whatever* intent, overturns The State in principle and, whatever his objective, may do so in fact.

The parliamentary state does provide for its own legal overthrow by "the people," who are also empowered to eradicate every individual liberty. When the United States Supreme Court in *Ex Parte Milligan* asserted that "the principles of constitutional liberty would be in peril, unless established by irrepealable law," it was speaking of a law that never was and never will be; the whole of the U.S. Constitution can be repealed as, of course, parts of it have been.

The right of "the people" to rebel, by ballot or bullet, presupposes that the citizen will rebel in behalf of his own liberties or, still more nobly, in conscientious behalf of another man's. But what if conditions should obtain in which most of the people have been trans-

formed into Hamilton's beast? Transported by fright—
and the hatred of the frightful—great majorities have
suppressed all liberty (including their own) in their
panic. They have called for Caesars—and got them.
They have denominated every deviation treason and
made the denomination stick. And not only in distant
times or places, and not necessarily by means of government except as an ancillary, and sometimes reluc-
tant, ally. Dwight Eisenhower was as far from being
a Caesar as a chief of State could be, but it was during
the American terror of the 1950's that Claude Bourdet,
the distinguished French editor, asked for his single
sharpest impression of an extended visit to the United
States, replied, "An American can say or do anything
as long as he begins by saying, 'I hate Communism,' "
—and an American trade union official, caught with
his hand in the till, said, "I was using the money to
fight Communism."

Liberty is at the mercy of a much more formidable
force even than The State power. Custom (as every
social philosopher has observed) is both weightier and
speedier than law. If we define liberty no more narrowly
than deviation from the behavior of the community in
general, we know how effectively the outraged community may smother dissent under the great wet blanket
of its hostility. Let it be carried away by fear and anger,
and state and local statutes and ordinances will almost
invariably outrun repressive federal law in their fervor
to curtail and suppress; and even without benefit of
statute or ordinance, it will come down on the devia-
tionist like a wolf pack on a one-sheep fold. Jefferson
defended the exclusion of government action in the area
of religion on the ground that religious extremists would
be "laughed out of doors"; but the Nineteenth Century

Mormons, assaulted and murdered wherever they went, hounded westward from town to town and state to state, and finally subjected in Utah by the U.S. Army, did not feel that they had been laughed out of doors.

The record of American "frontier justice," of vigilanteism and lynch law, is the historical scandal—and televised delight—of the world. In the past, as in the present, The State's power was often (if it arrived in time) invoked against the illegal exercise of social power; with the individual haplessly dependent for his rights, or even his life, on the preponderance of the massed violence of the government over the massed violence of the mob. Indeed, such is the melancholy history of mass fury that the case can be made that the power of The State alone, even though it be totalitarian *in posse,* is the individual's only protection against society turned (so to say) posse.

We speak of Hitler's and Stalin's tyranny, of their destruction of the liberties of the people; but hear Hannah Arendt in *The Origins of Totalitarianism:*

In view of the unparalleled misery which totalitarian regimes have meant to their people—horror to many and unhappiness to all—it is painful to realize that they are always preceded by mass movements and that they command and rest upon mass support up to the end. Hitler's rise to power was legal in terms of majority rule and neither he nor Stalin could have maintained the leadership of large populations, survived many interior and exterior crises, and braved numerous dangers of the relentless intra-party struggles if they had not had the confidence of the masses. Nor can their popularity be attributed to the victory of masterful and lying propaganda over ignorance and stupidity. For the propaganda of totalitarian

83

movements which precede and accompany totalitarian regimes is invariably as frank as it is mendacious, and would-be totalitarian rulers usually start their careers by boasting of their past crimes and carefully outlining their future ones.

The mendacious propaganda of totalitarian movements, bringing totalitarian regimes to power, is historically dramatic. Much less dramatic, much more commonplace, and much more durably ruinous of liberty is the settled custom of the society. No law and no government are involved in the Negro's making way for the white man on the sidewalk (or anywhere else) in the American South; in the inadmissibility of a Jew to a medical school or a suburb; or in the inability of a professing Communist (in the United States) to obtain a hearing or a hall in which he might make himself heard. It is not likely that the disadvantaged Negro or Jew, given his liberty, would use it to incite revolution; or that the Communist, if he so used it, would constitute a clear and present danger to The State. The persistent and pervasive enemy of liberty is the Way of Life acceptable to the culture generally, and it needs no statute, decree, proclamation, or indoctrination to effect its instinctive ends.

Liberty is the liberty of one man or it is not liberty at all, and I do not see how the issue will ever emerge from its welter of contradictions and self-contradictions until we talk about *the person* instead of *the people*. *The people* may lose their liberties by usurpation or incursion (or by abdicating them, as President Truman thought the Americans were doing when he vetoed the Internal Security Act of 1950). But they are less likely to lose theirs (or we ours) by usurpation or incursion than I mine. For they (or we) have recourses, legal and illegal, which are denied me when I stand alone. Standing alone, I am obnoxious. Liberty is the liberty of one obnoxious man.

Almost all societies are almost always sufficiently libertarian for the orthodox. It is not the Young Man of the Year who is, or is likely to be, in trouble. Liberty's first and last test is its application to those we suspect, to those we dislike, to those we dread, to those we detest; to those, as Justice Holmes said, whose thought (or act, or appearance) we hate. Thus the rising hubbub against Supreme Court decisions "coddling" suspected criminals and protecting the rights of the "lawless" against the lawful powers of the police and the prosecutors; thus the determination of political conservatives to replace the coddling justices with "strict constructionists" ordinarily directed against the common criminal, the outrage of the community is turned with a special fervor on the social or ideological nonconformist, the challenger, the Negro or student militant with his non-negotiable demands and his threat to "close it down" (or burn it down); above all, against what the late Al Smith called "the wire-whiskered Bolshevik with a bomb in each hand."

In the United States suppression of the rights of the Communist—or the alleged Communist—is the clearest example of the inability of the law (even of the courts) to withstand the power of public opinion. The "McCarthy period" of the early 1950's saw many Americans silenced, and even stifled, by one United States Senator speaking on behalf of a frenzied constituency which was not even legally his, since the activating aberration was hardly confined to Wisconsin. The Government found itself impotent against the fantastic charge, for instance, that there were 215 Communists in the State Department. This shabby epoch ended in the downfall of the Senator, but only *when he attacked the Army*—an attack so far-fetched it finally turned public opinion, and the retired general in the White House, against him. But Joe McCarthy's soul goes marching on, in the persons of other politicians using the Congressional powers of investigation to "expose" the Red Menace and lay the foundations for repressive legislation.

A decade or so later Presidential candidate Richard M. Nixon explained his own conspicuous association with McCarthyism by saying, "I was very young then." But the evil that very young men do lives after them. In 1963 the American Institute of Public Opinion and the National Opinion Research Center found that 68% of the American people would not allow a Communist to make a speech; 66% would take his books out of the library; 90% would fire him from a defense plant job; 91% would fire him from a high school teaching post; 89% would fire him from a college professorship; 68% would fire him from a clerk's job in a store; 77% would take away his American citizenship; 61% would put him in jail; and 64% would give the government the right to eavesdrop on his, or anybody else's, telephone conversation in order to get evidence against Communists.

On June 5, 1961, the Supreme Court handed down two decisions, by that tremulous 5- to- 4 margin common in "Communist" cases, upholding the McCarran and Smith Acts, which, between them, required the Communist Party of the U.S.A. to register as a foreign-controlled agency of international Communism; and punished membership in any organization which the member "knows" advocates the overthrow of the government by force and violence. Protesting, on behalf of the four dissenters that the majority was, for the first time in American history, "banning an association because it advocates hated ideas," Justice Black recorded the date as "a fateful moment in the history of a free country." (Congress had already, in 1950, passed the McCarran Act over President Truman's veto.) In subsequent split decisions, the Court, with an altered personnel, reversed itself on some of the powers it had upheld, notably registration. It would seem that the fate of a free country—as Justice Black looked upon it—depends upon one vote by one man appointed to his post by the executive of The State, the President.

The libertarian philosophers and statesmen will not take me standing alone and (because I stand alone) obnoxious; only the libertarian theologian and an odd bird like Tolstoy or Thoreau. Among secular personages, it is they and their likes who, without much philosophical respectability, address themselves to the predicament of the solitary, they alone who confront the dilemma of one man and The State.[16] *They* are the true antithesis of Hobbes' absolutism; they hem and haw not; and they exclude themselves from the serious consideration of political theory by coming down on the side of purest anarchy.

Thoreau refused to pay his tax for the support of the Mexican War and slavery, spent a night in Concord jail, and was sprung by his friend Emerson, who paid his tax. (The legend is that when Emerson peered at him through the bars and said, "Whatever are you doing

---

[16]"All government," says the still stately, and once rock-ribbed, *London Times*, "is based on the illusion that the individual is powerless against the Government." Do our eyes deceive us? They do. The next sentence reads: "When *enough individuals* [italics mine.—Author] protest together, the strongest Government bends." *London Times*, May 20, 1968.

in *there?*" Thoreau replied, "Whatever are you doing out *there?*") "Unjust laws exist," Thoreau wrote in his *Civil Disobedience.* "Shall we be content to obey them, or shall we endeavor to amend them, and obey them until we have succeeded, or shall we transgress them at once? Men generally, under such a government as this, think that they ought to wait until they have persuaded the majority to alter them. They think that, if they should resist, the remedy would be worse than the evil. But it is the fault of the government itself that the remedy is worse than the evil. *It* makes it worse."

If an injustice (he goes on) is part of "the necessary friction of the machine of government . . . then you may consider whether the remedy will not be worse than the evil; but if it is of such a nature that it requires you to be the agent of injustice to another, then, I say, break the law . . . It is not my business to be petitioning the governor or the legislature any more than it is theirs to petition me; and, if they should not hear my petition, what should I do then? But in this case The State has provided no way; its very constitution is the evil. . . . I do not hesitate to say that those who call themselves abolitionists should at once effectively withdraw their support, both in person and property, from the government of Massachusetts and not wait till they constitute a majority of one before they suffer the right to prevail through them. Moreover, any man more right than his neighbors constitutes a majority of one already. . . ."

So our majority of one "quietly declares war with The State, after my fashion," assured as to the eventuation: "a minority is powerless while it conforms to the majority; it is not even a minority then; but it is irresistible when it clogs by its whole weight. . . ." But he isn't all that confident, and in the end he wonders whether "democracy, such as we know it, [is] the last improvement possible in government. Is it not possible to take a step further toward recognizing and organizing the rights of man? There will never be a really free and enlightened state, until The State comes to recognize the individual as a higher and independent power, from which all its own power and authority are derived, and treats him accordingly. . . ."

And when will that State be? Never. On this point "liberal" political theory is one with "conservative," the reformer with the standpat contemporary journalist, William Buckley: "That which is anarchic within me (which is very strong) tunes in strongly on the idea of a society in which people decide for themselves what taxes to pay, what rules to obey, when to cooperate and when not to with the civil authorities. But that which is reasonable within me, which I am glad to say most often prevails, recognizes that societies so structured do not exist, and cannot exist."

Henry David Thoreau's polemics have affected the course of history, certainly in the liberation of India. But they have not changed the nature of The State and its relationship to man, and the government of liberated India is no more The State Thoreau dreamed of than any other. The widespread application of his doctrine to the civil rights campaign in the United States has had, and is still having, a profound effect on American law and American culture. But it has had none whatever on *the supremacy of law;* although state and local statutes have been struck down at the federal level as unconstitutional, no judge and no court has upheld civil disobedience *to the Constitution.* The State which Thoreau pleased himself (as he said) to imagine is no more visible than it was a century ago, or twenty.

CHAPTER
VII

E. Pluribus Einheit

States differ, and differ radically, in regard to their forms of government and the extent to which the liberty of the individual is protected by law, and by government's adherence to the law. But in the rock-bottom respect of the ultimate power of The State there is no difference at all. The gulf is immense between Western democracy and the overt or covert tyranny of, say, the most liberal Communist regime, with its total control of mass communication and its restrictions on religion, art, education, association, and economic enterprise. But it is not an absolute gulf. Soviet travel limitations (especially of non-Communists) are far more repressive than American (especially of Communists), but the greatness of difference in degree does not constitute a difference of kind. I know of no penalty imposed upon deviation by one modern state or society, legally or customarily, that is not imposed by another upon some segment of its citizens, though the segments are not the same and the penalties are here lighter, there heavier.

In America (or Russia) the anguished cry is at once heard: "Do you mean to say that *we* are no different from *them?*" Only in this one respect, only in the last analysis (which we are trying to make here). Think of our national slogans and their univocal applicability to the most tyrannical of states: "E Pluribus Unum," "United We Stand," "In Union There Is Strength." Do they differ from Hitler's *Einheit?* Think closely and precisely of the late President Kennedy's most memorable words, "Ask not. . . ." and consider again that an Oriental (or an Occidental) despot could have uttered the identical phrases, with the identical meaning. And consider, too, that the contrary of those words would plunge The State into a commitment to its own dissolution.

Whatever *any* State has to do—or in its less than infinite wisdom believes (or says it believes) it has to do—will be done and has been done. The World War II deportation of the Nisei from the American West Coast was done. The British Government's exclusion of its own citizens of Asian origin was done, even more recently. The West German Government's seizure of a respected oppositionist periodical—in the name of protecting the morals of the young—was done, and right now. No one believes we have heard the last of the earnest segregationist, former Governor George Wallace of Alabama, who says in his continuing campaign for the American Presidency: "I would keep the peace if I had to keep 30,000 troops standing in the streets, two feet apart and with two-foot-long bayonets." "The peace" has been kept in this way, the way of liberty's denial, in "free countries" everywhere—as the always regrettable alternative to anarchy.[17]

The paralyzing prospect of anarchy goes back a long way. As a view of life it is at least as old as the Stoics of the Third Century B.C. Though it has independent roots in the England of Godwin, the France of Proudhon, and the Italy of Malatesta, its most powerful advocacy emanated (understandably enough) from the ferociously repressive conditions of Czarist Russia. Tolstoy was its theologian, its Thoreau; the gentle, optimistic Kropotkin and the wild Bakunin its theorists. They held that government's ultimate function was the maintenance of an unjust order that crushed individuality; take government away, and injustice would disappear. It would not follow that men would be unorganized; they would organize themselves voluntarily, in local communities and industries, with every man's consent, and on this voluntary basis maintain a truly associative society.

Some anarchists were terrorists, and the political assassins of the end of the Nineteenth Century all claimed the dread designation; it was the black flag of anarchy, not the red flag of communism, that represented the End of Everything to the Victorian rich and their bourgeois royalty. But most anarchists were pacifists, and all of them socialist exponents of mutual aid. And one of the first acts of the "dictatorship of the proletariat" in Russia was to use artillery to destroy the anarchist headquarters in Moscow and suppress the anarchist movement (which had been sympathetic to the Russian

---

[17] The triumphant Gaullist slogan in the French elections of 1968, following the student uprising in Paris, was, *CONTRE L'ANARCHIE—Division-Impuissance.*

revolution). American law, without saying what an anarchist is, still forbids the immigration of foreign anarchists and provides for the deportation of anarchist aliens.

The classic advocates of anarchy as a system are trapped by a self-contradictory concept, and are necessarily romantics. Their no-State has no more substance, no more operability, no more *imaginability*, than Thoreau's; it too demands that men be angels. Its romanticism is evident in the divergence of its witting or unwitting adherents, who may reject the theory and accept the practices. They include not only the Martin Luther Kings, resting their case on the supremacy of God, but the most violent atheists; not only the revolutionary students of Paris (and elsewhere), but the man who until recently represented The State's most far-reaching abridgement of the liberty (even the lives) of its law-abiding citizens, General Hershey, former Director of the United States Selective Service, who, on another occasion, said he knew of no solution for the problem of conscientious objection in any large proportion of the men of military age; faced (at the Yale Law School) with the hypothetical question of what he would do if he were of draft age and found it morally impossible to support a war, the General replied: "I'd rather go to jail."

So amorphous is anarchy that it has room not only for terrorists, pacifists, Negro Christians, and generals, but also the deepest-dyed Tory. In the sunny groves of Orange County, California, probably the most conservative political diocese in America, the Santa Ana *Register* has been published for thirty years by the aged Raymond Cyrus Holles, who calls himself "a radical for freedom." Mr. Holles opposes taxation as "just plain stealing." "The. Government," he says, "ought to be supported on a strictly voluntary basis." Does that go for parks, post offices, police, and the schools? Absolutely. *And* for conscription, and immigration laws and the outlawry of Communists. Mr. Holles, says Columnist Arthur Hoppe, has carried Conservatism to its logical extreme, and "the more you talk to him, the more he sounds like an anarchist."

To say that no State has ever supported the right of revolution—or of anarchy—is not literally accurate. Four great states, the U.S.A., the U.S.S.R., Great Britain, and France, not only supported it but demanded it, *ex post facto,* of every soldier and bureaucrat of Nazi Germany, under the Nuremberg Judgment of 1946 that required the hanging of those convicted as "war criminals." The *New York Times* hailed the decision of the four-power tribunal as historic, "proclaiming new legal rules and standards which now become integral parts of international law . . . National sovereignty has been superseded by the superior sovereignty of international law and international organization, which takes jurisdiction not only over states and nations but also over individuals responsible for their governments and policies. And every kind of crime connected with . . . aggressive war is subject to the same authority, which accepts no excuse of either 'superior orders' or the peril of disobedience." The high Nazi officials had all pleaded superior orders from Hitler, the head of State, who was dead. The plea was rejected in advance; the Four-Power Agreement establishing the Tribunal asserted criminality "whether or not [the acts were] in violation of the domestic law of the country where perpetrated."

If the Nuremberg Judgment meant anything, it meant that the soldier (not to say the civilian) has to decide for himself whether or not he can obey an officer's (or an official's) legal order and be held responsible, even on pain of the death penalty, if he does obey the order and in doing so commits what subsequently may be held to have been a war crime, a crime against peace, or a crime against humanity. Here is prescribed the right, indeed the duty, not merely of civil, but of *military* disobedience. It may be impossible to imagine an army operating under such conditions—but it is easy to imagine what would happen if it tried. Nuremberg was, of course, a sham. None of the four great States which imposed the doctrine on the defeated Germans has adopted it for its own soldiery (and the new German *Wehrmacht* has also ignored it). When four American soldiers refused transfer to combat duty in Vietnam, on the ground that the war was "unjust, immoral, and illegal," Assistant General Counsel Frank A. Bartimo of the Department of Defense announced that they might be sentenced to death by a court martial—for doing what the Nuremberg Tribunal required a soldier to do under threat of death if he did not.

Besides the members of the Nuremberg Tribunal, the publisher of the Santa Ana *Register,* and the Director of Selective Service, anarchy may claim one other eminent advocate: the government of every existing State (whose anarchical condition invariably enjoys the support of nearly all of its citizens). National sovereignty is the state of being independent of any governance; in a word, anarchy. The recognition that all sovereigns live in the fabled state of nature *vis à vis* one another is as old as The State itself. Every Muscovite, every New Yorker, is under the city's ordinances; every city is under the statutes of the province or state; and every province or state is under the law of the land. But the land itself is under no law; if it accepts the "decisions" of the United Nations, it does so uncoerced and (in the case of a great power) uncoercible. And so deeply inbred is nationalism that the unilateral (i.e., anarchic) actions of nations are supported by nearly all of their people. The anarchy of the world has now been extended to the solar system. In 1969 the Congress of the United States memorialized the United States Space Administration to plant the American flag and no other (the United Nations flag had been suggested) on the moon. Earlier the Russians had dropped the Red flag of the U.S.S.R. on that unprotesting satellite.

Individual liberty is, and must be, the prerogative of The State because of The State's paramount function to preserve itself, i.e., its sovereignty. In 1931 the United States Supreme Court, in a case involving a divinity school professor who was denied citizenship because he refused to bear arms, held that though "we are a Christian people . . . we are a Nation with the duty to survive." We must, therefore, "go forward upon the assumption, and safely can proceed on no other, that unqualified allegiance to the nation and submission and obedience to the laws of the land, as well those made for war as those made for peace, are not inconsistent with the will of God." One is reminded of the genuine astonishment of the British soldiers of World War I who first saw the buttons on a German uniform bearing the inscription, *Gott mit uns,* since they themselves had been called to the colors for God and Country. What the Supreme Court said of the American nation could be said (and has been said) on behalf of every nation that has ever existed: it has the "duty" to survive.

Only once, so far as I know, has this "duty" been called into juridical question; and the question was not pursued, on or off the bench. In 1967 the Supreme Court struck down a provision of the Subversive Activities Control Act of 1950 that made it a crime for Communist Party members to work in a defense plant. It was held that the provision violated the freedom of association guaranteed by the First Amendment. Speaking for the Court, the then Chief Justice Warren said that "the phrase 'war power' cannot be invoked as a talismanic incantation to support any exercise of Congressional power which can be brought into its ambit." He went on: *"This concept of 'national defense' cannot be deemed an end in itself, justifying any exercise of legislative power designed to promote such a goal. Implicit in the term 'national defense' is the notion of defending those values and ideals which set this nation apart.* For almost two centuries, our country has taken singular pride in the democratic ideals enshrined in its Constitution, and the most cherished of those ideals have found expression in the First Amendment. It would indeed be ironic if, in the name of national defense, we would sanction the subversion of one of *those liberties*—the freedom of association—*which make the defense of the nation worthwhile."* [Italics Mine.—author] Neither of the two dissenting members of the Court touched on the doctrine that "the national defense cannot be deemed an end in itself." Nor has any learned comment on the case that has come to my attention. Even the chauvinist advocates of Mr. Justice Warren's impeachment failed to rise to the occasion on which their *bête noir* appears flatly to have rejected the dictum, "My country, right or wrong."

Liberty, then, is what The State allows in fulfilling its "duty to survive." The omelette *does* take precedence over the egg. How much power over the individual belongs to The State? The answer has to be: as much as The State deems necessary to preserve itself, including all. To talk about *responsible* or *limited* government is to talk about government hamstrung.[18]

But the preservation of The State is all things to all men. I do not endanger The State's very existence by throwing a rock through my neighbor's window or snatching his purse. The State is not dissolved so easily. What I endanger is its preservation in a certain condition generally characterized as order (or, platitudinously *and* more ominously, law and order). But order in human affairs is a chimerical thing, no easier to define than it is to achieve. Life is a tumult of accidents, frenzies, exaltations, and desperations. Men are not orderly. States—least of all in their relations with one another—are no more orderly than men.

What is social order? In one society it is chattel slavery, in another concentration camps. Present-day Spain provides imprisonment for those who publish anything "detrimental to the government, the state, the armed forces, and the interests of the country." ("Maybe we will be permitted to publish the weather report," said a Spanish journalist of this Franco statute.) In still another society social order may mean legalized prostitution, wide-open gambling, free access to firearms, racial or religious persecution, or even trial by lynch mob. The military junta on the right, the Revolutionary Committee on the left, when they suspend civil liberties, do so in the name of preserving or restoring order. In the center, the President of the United States summons the governors of the states to "a crusade for public order,

---

[18]In *The Spirit of Liberty* Judge Learned Hand, universally recognized as one of the greatest of contemporary jurists, said wryly (but univocally) that "liberty is so much latitude as the powerful choose to accord the weak."

in every sense of that phrase," to eliminate "crime in the streets." "No society," he says, "can tolerate attacks upon itself." True—and the invariable dictum of every democrat and of every dictator.

What is "an attack upon society?" My wartime dissent which gives "aid and comfort to the enemy?" My insistence upon taking my Saturday night bath in my own home? My letting my hair grow as long as Andrew Jackson's (in contravention of an anti-hippie ordinance of the City of New Orleans where General Jackson won his most famous battle)? We do not agree on a definition, my neighbor and I; and neither does the Supreme Court Justice and his neighbor on the bench. Consider the Fourteenth Amendment's prohibition of involuntary servitude. It is a dead letter as regards military conscription. But its protection of strikers—of the right not to work—was cemented into American public law by the National Labor Relations Act. The civilian employer *must* bargain with his collective employees. Fair enough, if the Fourteenth Amendment is to mean what it says. But the President "finds" that the striking railroad workers have created a national transportation emergency, and he threatens to seize the facilities and compel their continued operation; and collective bargaining ends with The State's power to knock the contending parties' heads together. So the General Strike in England ended in 1926—as it always has—at bayonet's point.

National Labor Relations Act or no National Labor Relations Act, public employees, civilian no less than military, are forbidden to strike by national, state, and local legislation.[19] But by the end of the 1960's the

---

[19]Thirty years after the passage of the N.L.R.A., postal union officials were still protesting that "labor without the right to strike is shackled. This is contrary to our *way* of life." (*New York Times*, Oct. 11, 1969.)

United States (and many other countries) had to put up with unthinkable stoppages, by certified public employees from garbage collectors to teachers, firemen, and policemen, and by employees in such vital services "affected with a public interest" as air and surface transport and even hospital and medical care; with the response of an ever increasing, and ever less effective, spate of prohibitory legislation.[20]

Do I similarly jeopardize the survival of The State by standing on a soapbox before a small audience, and actually crying up revolution? The commonest of Sunday afternoon diversions of my boyhood was to accompany my father to Washington Park to hear the wild men in "bughouse corner," off the ball field. A single policeman, Big Tom by name, was the entire representation of The State, swinging his club ferociously at the small children on the edge of the crowd when they made so much noise at play their fathers could not hear the revolutionaries rant. My father listened attentively every Sunday afternoon—and went right on voting the straight Republican ticket. These days the confrontation of Man v. The State appears in clearer outline, what with the disappearance of the solitary bughouser and his replacement by the massed mob wielding brickbats in confrontation with the massed nightsticks, buckshot, and bayonets of Big Tom's successors; a progression that demonstrates how "public order" and "public necessity" may be (and more often than not are) stretched to cover

---

[20]On October 7, 1969, Canada's largest city, Montreal, was "struck" by its 3,700 policemen, with (according to the *New York Times*) "near-anarchy as a result." After a day and a night of widespread looting, robbery, riot, and arson, and with one man killed and four wounded, the Provincial Government broke the strike by emergency legislation providing imprisonment and fines of up to $50,000 for continued absence from duty.

every great public and private passion against every last human liberty.

Zechariah Chafee, Jr., perhaps the foremost legal scholar in the First Amendment field, holds that no one "should be allowed to say whatever he wants anywhere and at any time. We can all agree from the very start that there must be some point where the government may step in . . ." Such points *seem* clear—and simple. The State may let me cry, "Fire!" in an empty theatre, but prohibits my doing so in a crowded one. (Or at least prohibits my doing so falsely; but then I shall be sure to insist that I smelled smoke, or thought I did.) I agree that the prohibition is proper. But as soon as I agree that freedom of speech is unprotected by the First Amendment in this one "extreme" circumstance, I have accepted the principle under which all liberty may be suppressed. A distinction is made (by Meiklejohn, among others) between *suppression* and *control*—a distinction which may or may not comfort the man who is told that his speech is simply being controlled. "The First Amendment," said Justice Holmes, ". . . cannot have been, and obviously was not, intended to give immunity to every form of language. . . . We venture to believe that neither Hamilton nor Madison, nor any other competent person, ever supposed that to make criminal the counselling of a murder would be unconstitutional interference with free speech."

Good enough—but have we not, then, taken our position with the absolute power of The State? The First Amendment, with its guarantees of freedom of speech, press, assembly, and petition, begins, "Congress shall make no law respecting an establishment of religion, or prohibiting the free exercise thereof . . ." The separation of Church and State in the United States is the first of all absolutes. Congress shall make no law *having anything to do with religion.* The only appropriate response is, Humbug.

True, the Supreme Court held, in 1961, that the requirement of "a belief in the existence of God" as a qualification for public office "unconstitutionally invades . . . freedom of belief and religion and therefore cannot be enforced." But it is also true that this same Supreme Court, whose Chief Justice uses a Bible to administer the oath of office to the President, continues to open its sessions with the words, "God save the United States and this honorable court." In 1969 the President established what theologian Reinhold Niebuhr called a "modern version of the king's chapel" by inaugurating divine services in the State-owned Executive Mansion. Every American coin is inscribed "In God We Trust." Every juror and witness in a lawsuit attests his devotion to truth in the name of God. The Pledge of Allegiance to the American flag puts the nation "under God."

Convicted under a Maryland blasphemy statute, an American was imprisoned in 1968 on the charge that he "did unlawfully use profanity by taking the Lord's name in vain." (There has been some progress; the 245-year-old statute invoked in this case originally called for the felon to be bored through the tongue for the first offense, branded with the letter B on the forehead for the second, and put to death without benefit of clergy for the third.) Churches and parochial schools receive government aid in the form of tax exemption and always have; public schools may release students for prayer, and must release students for Christmas. Congress provides state-employed chaplains to the Armed Forces, and one for each of its own houses, and prescribes exemption from military training and service on the ground of "religious belief." (In order to grant the exemption, Congress must decide that the applicant's belief is in fact religious; it must therefore distinguish between religion and non-religion; which is precisely what the First Amendment forbids it to do.)

So much for the first clause of the First Amendment *"Congress shall make no law . . ."* But what if the free exercise of my religion involves human sacrifice and the victim is willing? Congress says No. What if it involves my handling a poisonous snake? Congress says No. What if it involves polygamy? Congress says No. What if it forbids my being vaccinated or my drinking fluoridated water? Congress says No. What if it forbids my sending my child to school? Congress says No. What if it forbids me (or my children) access to information about contraception? Congress says No. What if it requires me to love my enemy and provide medical supplies to the civilians of North Vietnam? Congress says No. Every one of these cases (except the first) is real, contemporary, and commonly reported in the press, which also records that every one of these infringements on religious liberty has been upheld by the courts. The free exercise of religion has been denied Christian Scientists, Jehovah's Witnesses, Mormons, Amish, and members of the "peace churches"—just as a hundred years ago it was denied the farmer in Southern Ohio whose religious belief required him to succor a fugitive slave. Congress has made no end of laws respecting religion, and the courts have sustained them. The Supreme Court refused to stay an order that a sick woman be given a blood transfusion even though she *and her husband* refused it on the ground that it violated the Biblical injunction against "drinking blood." This is the same

Supreme Court that said: "If there is any fixed star in our constitutional constellation, it is that no official, high or petty, can prescribe what shall be orthodox in politics, nationalism, religion, or other matters of opinion or force citizens to confess by word or act their faith therein."

By word *or act*—there is the sticking point. I may believe—but I may not act upon my belief or do the things my belief requires of me. I am condemned *unless* I stand with the Pharisees, and they were condemned by Christ because "they say—and do not; Not all they that say, 'Lord, Lord,' shall enter the Kingdom . . . He that believeth on me, the things that I do, he shall do likewise." Let the law permit me to act on my religion and, as Jeremy Bentham put it long ago, you "arm every fanatic against all governments"; for "in the immense variety of ideas respecting natural and Divine law, cannot some reason be found for resisting all human laws?" Very probably; and so one of the two, Divine law or human law, must fall. One does, and that one is not the human law, which (in the United States Constitution) specifically protects not only religion but *the free exercise thereof.*

So, too, with reference to every other "absolute" right. Under the United States Uniform Code of Military Justice, Army counsel in the celebrated court-martial of Captain Howard B. Levy in 1967 argued successfully that a citizen under arms has the right to *think* as he will but not to act upon his thinking *or* utter his thought. The Post Office invades my privacy (if I am a suspect person) by putting a "mail-cover" on me, i.e., making a record of the sender's name and address, and place and date of postmark, of every letter I receive; and the Postmaster General of the United States says: "There's

105

no question in my mind that mail covers do, to some degree, invade individual rights . . . [However] I'm not ready, at this point, to talk about abolishing them." The same Post Office defends the interception of mail addressed to delinquent taxpayers—(a "sneaky, un-American, undemocratic Gestapo tactic," Senator Ralph Yarborough of Texas called it on the floor of the Senate) on the ground that an order of the Internal Revenue Service "has the same authority as a search warrant." And until a few years ago, when the Supreme Court, for the first time in American history, struck down a federal statute as a violation of the First Amendment, the Post Office itself opened printed matter addressed to Americans from Communist countries whether or not they were suspected persons.

My *truthful* statement about another man (unless he's a public figure) may be held criminal as slander or libel. The limitation of my right to label such products as foods and drugs—fought long and hard in the courts a generation or two ago—is now accepted as a proper State control. As every home owner knows who has come up against urban renewal or the construction of a freeway, my Fourth Amendment right to be secure "against unreasonable . . . seizure" is at the mercy of the supersedent right of eminent domain under which The State does the seizing and also determines the reasonableness of the seizure; and my concomitant security in my "effects" is at the mercy of The State's unlimited power to destroy me by taxation.

Nor is it possible to justify all these whips and scourges on the ground that the exercise of my liberty would injure another. The "unnatural"—that is, unpopular—"practice" of Mormon polygamy was religious, and it outraged the sensibilities of the monogamists who comprised almost the whole of American society; but it is hard to see how it injured them. The Christian Scientist was held to have injured others by his rejection of vaccination against epidemic disease; but it is hard to see how his rejection of medical care, say, for cancer, was an injury to others—unless The State is to decide that his family is injured when his family denies it. What if a bachelor orphan of what the law calls consenting age forms a homosexual attachment with another bachelor orphan of consenting age? What if a heterosexual bachelor who doesn't drive a car is a drunkard? Whom does he injure by his drinking? Himself? Is The State, then, to determine what constitutes injury to oneself? If so, may it not determine what I shall eat (and when, and how much) and drink (as it once did under Volstead) and read and hear, and whether I shall be permitted to go out of my house in the rain without an umbrella, and how hard a mattress I shall sleep on?

A reduction to absurdity, you say. But the absurdity, if there is such, is established in the principle that I am not free to do as I like (to use narcotics, for instance) when my doing so does not injure another. And if I may be restricted on the ground that what I do *might* injure another, then there is no possible limit at all to The State's power. I *might* do anything. I might kill a man with the gun the Second Amendment guarantees I have a right to possess. If I carry a baseball bat, I might use it to club a passerby as I go down the street to the playing field; if I study chemistry I might use my knowledge to concoct poisons or blow safes—so baseball and chemistry are swept under the ban, and only a paucity of imagination can set its ultimate limit.

CHAPTER
VIII

Who Says There's a Fire?

What is marvelous is not that Congress has made laws in violation of First Amendment freedoms, or that some of these invasions have or have not been struck down by the courts, but that the fundamental doctrine on which they are made and upheld or struck down continues to be disputed with unabated heat. The most learned men of the law continue to accuse one another, from the highest bench, of being the enemies of freedom or security. When the Supreme Court voted 5 to 4 that the Fifth Amendment protection against self-incrimination permitted the police to take a blood sample from a driver suspected of being drunk, Justice Black said it was "a strange hierarchy of values that allows the State to extract a human being's blood. . . ." Justices Black and Douglas said that "what happens under this law is typical of what happens in a police state," in dissenting from the opinion upholding New York's "Feinberg Act" requiring the dismissal of teachers belonging to subversive organizations. "The hallmark of a totalitarian regime," dissenting Justice Potter Stewart called the 5-to-4 conviction of a publisher of erotic books in 1966.

The ambiguity of freedom is epitomized, in the United States just now, by the lurid confusion attending "snooping," electronic and otherwise, by Government agencies. Federal statutes regarding the invasion of privacy are in utter conflict with one another and with state statutes. But what are statutes between friends? Former Senator Gruening of Alaska says (without refutation from any quarter) that the Internal Revenue Service, in order to install telephone "taps" in taxpayers' homes, disguises its agents as Bell Telephone workers and uses fake telephone company trucks. Senator Fong of Hawaii said several years ago that the Department of Justice was "bugging" suspected criminals as a matter of course, in spite of Congressional refusal to legalize its doing so. Senator Long of Missouri, having produced an admission by the Internal Revenue Service that it conducts a special school in snooping, conducted the following dialogue, in Congressional committee, with an IRS representative:

Long: Is there a special course in that school on teaching the use of burglar tools?

Owen B. Yung (Intelligence Division, IRS): There is, or was, up until this year a course in lockpicking.

Long: What would you use the art of lockpicking for?

Yung: For surreptitious entry.

Long: Well, that would still be breaking and entering, wouldn't it?

Yung: Technically, I guess so, sir.

Long: Violation of the law?

Yung: I wouldn't know, sir. I am not a lawyer.

But while statesmen and bureaucrats argue the secret surveillance of suspected criminals and tax-dodgers, there is no argument whatever on the snooping activities of one branch of the government. This is the so-called "security community," the FBI, the CIA, and the intelligence divisions of the Departments of State and Defense. So wholeheartedly is power thrust upon these agencies that "the indispensability of the Central Intelligence Agency to the security of the State" strips men of their protection against defamation, and even against murder. The courts recently dismissed the suit of an Estonian émigré leader against a CIA operative who called him a Soviet secret agent. The judge, though he found the function of the CIA "an esoteric subject," held that its activities should not be hampered "by a too strict application of legal principles, including the principles of libel and slander." Still more recently the U. S. Army dropped murder charges against a group of officers of its own Special Forces ("Green Berets") on the ground that the CIA refused to let its agents testify in the case.

The revelations of government (and private) prying, especially by highly sophisticated electronic devices, became so sensational in the late 1960's that former President Johnson addressed himself to the matter in his 1967 State of the Union message. "We should," he said, "protect what Justice Brandeis called 'the right most valued by civilized men'—the right to privacy. We should outlaw all wire-tapping, public and private, wherever and whenever it occurs, except when the security of the nation itself is at stake—and only then with the strictest safeguards. We should exercise the full reach of our constitutional powers to outlaw electronic 'bugging' and 'snooping.' "

. . . Except when the security of the nation itself is at stake. The echo of the words had hardly subsided when the Congress of the United States, with a whoop and a holler, and a handful of dismayed dissenters, passed the Omnibus Crime Control Act of 1968. Here for the first time in American history legal sanction was provided for telephone wiretapping and "bugging" (eavesdropping by hidden microphones) by federal, state, and local law enforcement officers investigating murder, robbery, "organized crime," "drug abuse," and "other offenses" involving danger to "life, limb, and property." A court order was required, and the subject had to be informed of its issuance—but only after the tap or the bug had been removed. Libertarian protests in both Houses were brushed aside by the argument (of the House Republican leader) that "there can be no further quibbling about the urgent need for tougher law enforcement legislation."

It all had a familiar ring: "There is no time to waste on hair-splitting over infringement of liberty," said the Washington *Post* on the occasion of Attorney General A. Mitchell Palmer's "Red raids" in 1919. Exactly fifty years later another Attorney General, John Mitchell, revealed that the FBI had ignored the Congressional requirement of a court order to listen in on the conversation of youth leaders indicted for allegedly inciting riots at the Democratic National Convention of 1968 —*and would go on doing so.* "While it may be appropriate," said Mr. Mitchell, "for Congress to establish rules limiting the investigative techniques which the

Executive may employ in enforcing the laws that Congress has enacted, a serious question exists as to the power to restrict the President's power to gather information which he deems necessary to the proper exercise of powers which the Constitution confers on him alone. If the Congress cannot tell the President whom he should employ to direct the Army, there is a strong basis to argue that Congress cannot tell the President what means he may employ to obtain information which he needs to determine the proper deployment of his forces . . . The President . . . has the constitutional power to authorize electronic surveillance to gather intelligence information concerning domestic organizations which seek to attack and subvert the Government by unlawful means."

"For the first time in American history," said an attorney for men upon whom the FBI had snooped, "a member of the President's Cabinet has publicly, and proudly, stated that he has, in open violation of his oath of office, taken the law into his own hands." But only the candor was new. Prior to his assassination, Senator Robert F. Kennedy and FBI Director J. Edgar Hoover had tangled, inconclusively, on the question of who had authorized the "bugging" of whom during the former's tenure as Attorney General. There were rumors that the late Martin Luther King had been under secret surveillance—rumors steadfastly denied by both Kennedy and Hoover. A year after the King and Kennedy assassinations, FBI agents on the witness stand admitted that they had maintained electronic eavesdropping on King for several years. Had Kennedy known? Hoover, who had once called King "the most notorious liar in the country," permitted the Justice Department to reiterate his standard testimony that every secret eavesdrop by the FBI had been authorized in writing by the Attorney General in advance. The clamor of the press to see the written order in the King case was unavailing.

. . . *Except when the security of the Nation itself is at stake.* "The security of the country takes precedence over all First Amendment freedoms," Maximilian W. Kempner writes in *The Supreme Court and the Establishment and Free Exercise of Religion*—a doctrine which sweeps away every liberty and is nowhere seriously challenged. And it makes no difference whether The State is a "good" one or a "bad" one, the principle of self-preservation abides intact and inviolable. The absolute rights men—the Blacks and the Meiklejohns—concede that overthrow might, or (under conditions of extreme tyranny) would and should occur. But their argument for liberty unconfined is invariably based on the postulate that this is the very means of preserving The State—at least the free State. And it is certainly true historically that nations like England, with its Magna Carta, or the United States, with its Bill of Rights, have proved more resistant to revolution than a thoroughly repressive tyranny like Czarist Russia.

That the cure of the ills of the free society is more freedom is a cherished concept from which the inference is irresistible that there are States or governments worthy of preservation, and others unworthy, and that those that are overthrown by the most desperate exercise of freedom (namely, revolution) ought to be. But no government has yet been found that considered itself unworthy and, as a consequence, took no measures for its security. Thus it is, as Officer Sweeney lamented, that the very government against which my rights are guaranteed by the Constitution determines the conditions under which it may circumscribe my rights.

"Who," Hamilton asks in *The Federalist*, "is to be the judge of the *necessity* and *propriety* of the laws to be passed? . . . I answer . . . that the national government . . . must judge, in the first instance, of the proper exercise of its powers, and its constituents in the last." And if it passes tyrannical laws? Why, "there is then no resource left but in the exertion of that original right of self-defense which is paramount to all positive forms of government." But it is here, as everywhere, "the people" who will defend themselves; and this is not the issue. The issue is one man—one Nisei deported by the U. S. Army because of his (or his father's, or his grandfather's) national origin, or I myself, all alone and confronted by the community's power in the person of Officer Sweeney the night the town was on fire.

The town is on fire—and that is enough for Officer Sweeney. But is it in fact? And if it is, is the fire so widespread and so far out of control as to jeopardize the town's existence? Who says so? Before I surrender my sacred liberties, I have to be convinced. If Officer Sweeney has the time—*if* he has the time, in so terrible an emergency—he will describe the extent of the fire to me in convincing detail, and I (as a reasonable man) will be convinced and at once forego my bath and report for fire duty.

But the emergency most commonly affecting my liberty is not local, but national, and the security in jeopardy is the national security. Officer Sweeney is then President Sweeney of the United States, elected by me (or perhaps over my opposition) to minister to my sovereign needs. Unfortunately (as he himself says), he alone understands the extent of the emergency, which is beyond my inexpert and uninformed comprehension. (And even beyond that of the courts. Attorney General

Mitchell, in his assertion of the absolute right of the President to use electronic surveillance, said that it "should not be subject to judicial review.") Still more unfortunately (as President Sweeney has his deputy tell me), the interest of national security prevents his informing me. "Look," said Assistant Defense Secretary Arthur Sylvester to American reporters in Saigon, "if you think any American official is going to tell you the truth, then you're stupid." Mr. Sylvester went on to explain that it is the inherent right of government "to lie to save itself," and that the nation's leaders are justified in lying to its people when the national security is threatened.

So, when the presumed holocaust is of national dimension, in the interest of security I am first of all denied the right to know that there is a fire or how formidable it is—and then denied the rest of my rights because there's a formidable fire. So complex, recondite, and delicate are the matters affecting security that my ministers must be my rulers; and if there's a war on and I criticize their war policies, even on the basis of expert information available to, say, a Senator, they invoke the nation's wrath against me by accusing me of giving aid and comfort to the enemy.

"An idle man who wants his politics done for him, will have them done for him," said the British historian Bagehot. In the age of kings, soldiers said, "We know enough if we know that we are the king's subjects." Only *he* knew what was right and wrong and what should be done, and *our* only responsibility was to do as he said. "When our country is in a position of crisis," said former President Eisenhower, "there is only one thing a good American can do, and that is support the President." When President Johnson's Secretary of State

lost his cool at a press conference, he told the corre-
spondents: "There gets to be a point where the question
is: whose side are you on? Now I'm Secretary of State,
and I'm on our side. None of your newspapers or
broadcasting apparatuses are worth a damn unless the
United States succeeds. They are trivial compared to
that question . . ." But a free government is founded
upon the people's consent; if consent is to be uninformed or deceived, is it consent? Not in the common
criminal law. And if consent consists of nothing but
supporting the President, what is the difference between
a government with consent and a government without
it? The "Presidential War" replaces the "King's war."

In 1966 Chairman J. W. Fulbright of the Senate
Foreign Relations Committee said that the Senators of
the United States "have only ourselves to blame" for
signing "a blank check" on President Johnson's Vietnam policy. The check was signed, he said, on August
7, 1964, when the so-called Gulf of Tonkin Resolution
authorized the President to take "all necessary steps to
repel any armed attack against the forces of the United
States and to prevent further aggression." (The Resolution served as "the functional equivalent of a declaration of war," in the State Department's view.) Mr. Fulbright said he had supported the Resolution "because
I was confident that President Johnson would use our
endorsement with wisdom and restraint"—but he added
that his support was "a source of neither pleasure nor
pride to me today." Two years—and thirty thousand
casualties later—leading Senators charged the Administration with having provoked the North Vietnamese
attack (on two U. S. destroyers) which gave rise to the
Resolution.

How can men suppose that unlimited power can be

relied upon to limit itself? J. S. Mill thinks that dictatorship, freely given such power for a strictly limited time period, "can only be excused, if, like Solon or Pittacus, the dictator employs the whole power he assumes in removing the obstacles which debar the nation from the enjoyment of freedom." This is the same great libertarian who thought that barbarians were properly governed by a despot, hopefully a good despot like Akbar or Charlemagne; now he hopes that civilized men will have the good fortune to have a dictator like Solon or Pittacus.

But the alternative to "the blank check" is the preservation of the people's (if not the person's) liberty at the risk of the nation's destruction from without or within. The first of the two evils is generally the more terrifying. "Safety from external danger," Hamilton wrote in the great debate over the adoption of the Constitution, "is the most powerful director of national conduct. Even the ardent love of liberty will, after a time, give way to its dictates. The violent destruction of life and property incident to war, the continual effort and alarm attendant on a state of continual danger, will compel nations the most attached to liberty to resort for repose and security to institutions which have a tendency to destroy their civil and political rights. To be more safe, they at length become willing to run the risk of being less free."

Should nations, then, weigh these grim considerations in the decision to go to war? But *nations* no longer "go to war." In 1950 we found ourselves inextricably involved in a magnificent shoot-out which President Truman at the time called a "United Nations police action," and which, only after the fact, was recorded as the Korean War. *Governments* go to war now—as they did in ancient days, when citizens were mere subjects—and the people, in whose name they govern, have no voice, direct or indirect. The undeclared war eliminates the nation's painful choice to be more safe at the risk of being less free. But thirty years ago, when it was still the fashion to go to war by declaring it, a 1937 Gallup Poll found that 71% of the American people were in favor of Congressman Louis Ludlow's amendment to the Constitution providing that, "except in the event of an invasion of the United States or its territorial possessions and attack upon its citizens residing therein, the authority of Congress to declare war shall not become effective until confirmed by a majority of all votes cast therein in a nation-wide referendum." The "Ludlow Amendment," though the overwhelming majority of the American people wanted it, was kicked around in Congress until it disappeared from sight. Its opponents were not only Congressmen, but all the senior officials of the executive branch of the government and most of the leading figures in the world of international affairs. Their argument was a simple one: should there be a national emergency—even without an attack such as was to occur at Pearl Harbor in 1941—it would take too much time to inform and persuade the people to approve a declaration of war. Meanwhile the foreign enemy would have the advantage. Only Congress was expert and expeditious enough to make the decision.

But that was thirty years ago. Nowadays only the President is sufficiently expert and expeditious to make the decision. The undeclared war and "the blank check" have taken the place of even Congressional decision, and it is almost unimaginable that so specific a restraint as the Ludlow Amendment would be proposed (much less adopted) today. What was proposed (and adopted)

119

instead, five years after the Tonkin Resolution, was still another Resolution holding that "it is the sense of the Senate that a national commitment by the United States results only from affirmative action taken by the legislative and executive branches . . ." This toothless supplication, in no way binding upon the President, had as its "purpose" the "restoration of Constitutional balance" between the two branches. So far had an ever more republican country come from the settled conviction of its founding fathers (in *The Federalist*) that the "tendency of legislative authority to absorb every other . . . in governments purely republican is almost irresistible." Against the Supreme Court, Congress has always ultimately prevailed; against the Executive it has ultimately fallen.

But it would be gross oversimplification to conclude that The State's power is the President's—or *Congress'*. It lies, here and there, in bits and pieces, throughout the government establishment, and outside the government establishment. And the government, in the great nation-state, has become so immense that no one man can be said to govern; certainly not the President of the United States. Not only does he have to persuade an ordinarily suspicious Congress to grant him power, but within the executive agencies (whose head he is) major decisions are obviously made, and major steps taken, without his knowledge. Thus there is reason to doubt that President Eisenhower was dissembling when we denied that there was a U-2 espionage flight over the Soviet Union until the Soviets produced the flier they had shot down. President Kennedy, after the CIA had trained an army to invade Cuba and staged the invasion attempt at the Bay of Pigs, told a confidant that he wished the secret agency could be "taken to pieces and the pieces scattered to the winds"; and President Johnson likewise lamented the secret subvention of American student groups by the same agency. In his recently published book, *The Pentagon,* Pulitzer Prize winner Clark Mollenhoff develops in great detail the thesis that the Department of Defense is "now a law unto itself—beyond the control of Congress, the Supreme Court, or the President."[21]

It is a truism that "it is of the nature of war" (as the authors of *The Federalist* wrote) "to increase the executive at the expense of the legislative authority." Congressmen who do not want to be called traitors find themselves helpless to restrain the power of the President and the powers (apparently independent of the Presidency) of the great executive departments. Senator Fulbright's lament over "the blank check" is underscored, in even more pitiful terms, by other opponents of the Vietnam war. Offering an amendment to a military appropriation bill to forbid the continuation of the "immoral" bombing without a formal declaration of war, Senator Joseph S. Clark of Pennsylvania called the amendment (which had no chance of adoption) "a new means of Congressional protest." "I was looking," he said, "for something more we could do than write letters to the President or deliver speeches." Many a constituent who has written letters to his Congressman could sympathize with the Senator.

Every national emergency—real or pretended, fomented, imagined, or miscalculated as such—has always

---

[21]"Meanwhile, however, the White House, according to Republican Senators, has been preventing representatives of the opposition [to the deployment of the Anti-Ballistic Missile System] from seeing President Nixon—a policy that has only contributed to the new adamant stand of the opposition." (*New York Times,* July 7, 1969).

had a devastating effect upon individual liberty. If patriotism is the last refuge of a scoundrel, it is the first of a despot. The most spectacular such instance, in our time, is the burning of the German Reichstag a week before the election which gave Hitler absolute power. The Nazis called it the beginning of a Communist revolution, and the day after the fire Hitler obtained from President Hindenburg a decree "for the Protection of the People and the State," suspending the seven sections of the Weimar Constitution which guaranteed liberties. The terror of Bolshevism threw the German people into the arms of Hitler. Subsequent evidence is persuasive that the Nazis themselves planned and executed the arson.

But something like it, under similar conditions, is not unimaginable here or anywhere else. The Alien and Sedition Acts—which Supreme Court Justice William O. Douglas calls "the first reign of terror in this country"—were passed in 1798, when war with France seemed imminent, and continued in force until after Jefferson's election in 1800. After the fall of Fort Sumter in 1860 President Lincoln suspended the right of *habeas corpus* and ordered arrest without warrant and imprisonment without trial. The Supreme Court condemned the suspension as unconstitutional, but it was helpless against the President and the military authority. Lincoln went right on exercising the power, saying that "certain proceedings are constitutional when in case of rebellion or invasion the public safety requires them, which would not be constitutional when, in the absence of rebellion or invasion, the public safety does not require them." (Long after the fact, Congress authorized the President to suspend the writ.) So, too, in the case of the Emancipation Proclamation, though it never came before the court; widely attacked as an usurpation of power, it had (Lincoln himself said later) "no constitutional or legal justification, except as a military measure."

Hysterical peoples—like hysterical persons—may not be expected to know that they are hysterical. And when they recover, they are unenthusiastic about being told of the things they did. Thus the defeated Germans; thus the victorious Americans; thus all peoples everywhere. (The deportation of the Nisei from the U. S. West Coast in 1942 does not play a prominent role in modern history textbooks.) In the First World War, it was criminal in the United States, according to Professor Zechariah Chafee, in *The Blessings of Liberty,* "to advocate heavier taxation instead of bond issues, to state that conscription was unconstitutional (though the Supreme Court had not yet held it valid) . . . to urge that a referendum should have preceded our declaration of war, to say that war was contrary to the teachings of Christ. Men were punished for criticizing the Red Cross and the Y.M.C.A., while under the Minnesota Espionage Act it was held a crime to discourage women from knitting by the remark, 'No soldier ever sees these socks.' It was in no way necessary that these expressions of opinion should be addressed to soldiers or men on the point of enlisting or being drafted. Most judges held it enough if the words might conceivably reach such men." After the martial spasm, Chief Justice Charles Evans Hughes wondered, "in view of the precedents now established, whether constitutional government as hitherto maintained in this Republic could survive another great war even victoriously waged."

The Supreme Court defied Lincoln in vain. It did not even defy President Wilson. Congress gave him every power he pressed for, and where there was any question raised the judiciary sustained him. Objection to conscription as repugnant to the First Amendment guarantee of religious freedom was brushed aside, in *Arver v. United States* (1918) with the statement that it was too unsound to require rebuttal. And the most Olympian of all libertarians, Justice Oliver Wendell Holmes, upheld the conviction of a citizen for writing and circulating an anti-conscription leaflet, saying (for the unanimous Court) that "when a nation is at war many things that might be said in time of peace are such a hindrance to its effort that their utterance will not be endured so long as men fight . . . No court can regard them as protected by any constitutional right." The other "great dissenter" of that day, Justice Louis D. Brandeis, in a later case, said: "Only emergency can justify repression." The omission of "only" makes the point here, without changing the meaning of the dictum.

The circumscription of liberty in the name of national emergency has a way of outliving the emergency. The U. S. Sedition Act of 1917 provided for the punishment of anyone who might obstruct the sale of war bonds, incite insubordination, discourage recruiting, "willfully utter, print, write, or publish any disloyal, profane, scurrilous, or abusive language about the form of government of the United States, or the Constitution . . . or the flag . . . or the uniform of the Army or Navy . . . or bring the form of government . . . or the Constitution into contempt . . . or advocate any curtailment of production in this country of anything necessary or essential to the prosecution of the war." (The American Civil Liberties Union came into being to fight the use of the Act as an unconstitutional violation of the First Amendment.) The 1917 Act saw service in World War

II, and was still on the books when it was amended during the Korean War to remain in effect "until six months after the termination of the national emergency proclaimed by President Truman December 16, 1950." That emergency has not yet been "terminated" and the Act has never been repealed. "This is no longer a War-time Sedition Act," said the ACLU long after Korea. "Although framed in those terms, it is for all intents and purposes a permanent Sedition Act." In 1933 the Reichstag suspended the German Constitution and handed absolute power to Hitler *for a period of four years;* the power lasted twelve, until the death of Hitler and the Third Reich. Lenin's "war communism" was to have lasted five years after the Bolshevik seizure of power because "suppression is still necessary during the transition from capitalism to Communism"; the five years have become fifty.

In the name of never-ending emergency, martial law on Taiwan or "Nationalist China" has sustained the Chiang despotism during the entire twenty-year history of a "nation" which holds a great power's seat on the Security Council of the United Nations. In the Republic of South Korea, rescued from the threat of Communist tyranny by the "U. N. police action" of the 1950's, the mention of the name of Pablo Picasso—or any other Communist—is illegal. Statutes dealing with national emergency are commonly drawn so loosely as to permit any State action whatever. The Greek Constitution promulgated by the Papadopoulos dictatorship provides that the press is free unless it "creates defeatism." Article 30 of the French Penal Code, giving regional prefects almost unlimited power to investigate subversion, provides for the dispersal of any gathering that *could* lead to revolution and bans organizations that advocate violence. Article 190 of the Soviet Penal Code forbids "spreading of defamatory inventions against the Soviet State and participation in group activities harmful to public order."

Although the Preamble to the Constitution of the United States does not explicate the powers of any department in the Government, the Supreme Court has often cited its wording (especially the "general welfare" clause) in support of its decisions. The Preamble commits the Government to *—inter alia—*"insure domestic tranquillity." Could Congress have had domestic tranquility in view when it passed the 1950 Internal Security Act providing for detention camps (six are known to have been set up) for the internment of persons suspected of *probably* engaging in espionage or sabotage in time of war, insurrection, or "internal security emergency?" Never before had Americans been threatened with imprisonment for *probably* being criminals—except for the detention of the Nisei in 1942. But with "crime in the streets" rampant in 1969, President Nixon, after one month in office, asked Congress for authority to take action in the District of Columbia "whereby dangerous hard-core recidivists could be held in temporary pretrial detention when they have been charged with crimes and when their continued pre-trial release presents a clear danger to the community." This was another never-before. The presumption of innocence (until proof of guilt) is an established principle of American law; but so is the authority of the Government to "insure domestic tranquillity."

True, the history of national emergency has been much less baleful in traditionally free than in unfree societies. No reasonably objective historian would attempt to strike a balance between the suppression of

Constitutional rights under Lincoln and the repressions of the Nazis or the Bolsheviks. The grievous record of the Wilson Administration, with the mass imprisonment of Socialists and the lynching of conscientious objectors in the "virginal fervor" of America's first great foreign war, are as nothing to the massacres of Hitler and Stalin. And the Second World War was marked by so little repression (censorship was voluntary, and there were journals which never complied with it) that the Nisei deportation is made all the more spectacular by contrast. What is more, the free society, if it loses or surrenders much of its liberty to its own government, shows a salubrious tendency to regain a great deal, or even all, of it. But that is not the point. The point is two-fold. First, every society, however free, does come under the heel of The State power, however gently this or that State may tread. And, second, though liberty is recovered, by the time it is recovered I may be gone, and *my* liberty with me.

CHAPTER

IX

Hell or High Water

The Hobbesian doctrine of the indivisibility of sovereignty (he used it to argue for absolute monarchy) is as good a way as any of demonstrating that the affirmation of liberty is (just as Creon says) "the ruin of cities." Man is to The State (or the individual to society) as the states or provinces are to the nation. The divided sovereignty of the Articles of Confederation brought the United States to the point of collapse, and the unworkability of the system was so clear that a Constitution, reposing much greater sovereignty in the central government, was adopted. But the rights, that is, the liberty reserved to the separate states (slavery in particular) led to the Civil War and (as it appeared) the transfer of substantial sovereignty to Washington. What we are witnessing in our time, in the civil rights struggle, appears to be the slow death throes of the states, exemplified by such commonplace newspaper headlines as: U. S. Threatens Aid Cutoff to Alabama. The more homely way of stating the proposition is that somebody in the family has to wear the pants. The reason why The State would fall to pieces if it acknowledged absolute, inalienable rights is that the uncoerced unanimity of its citizens would be required for its operation.

The unanimity presupposed by liberty would have to be real unanimity, representing the free choice of each and every individual, and not hypothetical or customary consensus, or the "dead man's obedience" of the soldier who (even though he may be a volunteer) disobeys his officer at the peril of his liberty or his life. But true unanimity in a constituted society of many millions is inconceivable. No community, even in the absence of emergency, could withhold action until every member had made up his mind. A nation of two hundred million wise men would be hamstrung by the dissent, or merely by the dilly-dallying, of one fool. John Stuart Mill sought to alleviate the difficulty by allowing an increased suffrage, with a graduated number of votes, to the individual of "mental superiority"; assuming that Demos would agree, and that mental superiority could be determined in matters of morals and politics, the essential difficulty inherent in what Mill called "the tyranny of the majority" would remain: those who lost the election, be they the many with few votes or the few with many, would in essence have lost their liberty when a matter affecting their liberty was at issue.

The one nation-State in all history—so far as I have been able to discover—that actually tried to operate on the basis of unanimity (or absolute liberty) was Poland in the Seventeenth and Eighteenth Centuries. The Polish state literally destroyed itself in the process, and in doing so brought on (in considerable part) the agonies of the modern world. Poland was not, of course, a democracy, but an elective monarchy in fact ruled by the *sejm* (parliament) of the *szlachta* class (military landowning gentry) which comprised perhaps 10% of the country's population. (The rest of the populace had no voice in their governance, and no prescribed rights.) On the assumption of the absolute political equality of every Polish gentleman who was assigned a place above the line, the *liberum veto* (free vote) was adopted, requiring that every measure introduced into the *sejm* must receive a unanimous vote to pass. With one member's *"Nie pozwalam,"* (I disapprove) the measure died. Subsequently the *liberum veto* was extended to dissolve or "explode" the *sejm*—something that happened to forty-five out of fifty-five parliaments between 1652 and 1772.

The "country"—that is, the *szlachta*—was so predictably populated by needy and corruptible aristocrats that it was no great problem to find one member of the *sejm* to vote against any measure for a consideration, and the unabating struggle of Russia, Austria, and Prussia to devour paralyzed Poland introduced the decisive element of external corruption again and again. The struggle of patriot reformers against the *liberum veto* was futile. The monstrosity expired only with the expiration of Poland itself. After the last of its three partitions among the great powers in 1796, the Polish nation disappeared from the map of Europe for more than a century.

On two other notable occasions in history the attempt to maintain peace was similarly wrecked by the principle of divided sovereignty. The requirement of a unanimous vote by the Council of the League of Nations in all decisions of substance was the death of that organization when Germany and Japan "walked out," thus permitting Mussolini to defy the League and conquer Ethiopia in the early '30's. The history of the United Nations to date has run a similar course, with the great powers employing the veto to maintain their "liberty of action." On February 5, 1962, Prime Minister Macmillan of England put the facts of life plainly, if painfully, to the House of Commons:

The [U.N.] is not a sovereign body. It is not even an alliance. . . . It is an association of sovereign states whose sovereignty is especially emphasized by the Charter. . . . The whole foundation on which the U.N. was built has been undermined [by the Cold War]. . . . The U.N. can never be made to work unless political conditions can be created in the world which allow the Council to operate, not for perpetual propaganda purposes, not as a body permanently divided, but as a team. . . ."

It is not only the veto that immobilizes the U.N., but the Charter provision (like the League Covenant's) forbidding the organization to intervene in the "internal affairs" of any of its sovereign members. Sovereign Germany may massacre *its* Jews, the sovereign Soviet Union *its* kulaks, without violating any sovereign right of the League (or the U.N.) even to address itself to the matter; precisely as each of the antebellum Southern states enslaved *its* Negroes, with the "United" States helpless under a Constitution which reserved to the separate states their liberties *qua* states. A century after its resolution on this battlefield the American Civil War continues; the weight of arms provided a triumph for undivided sovereignty at Appomattox, but more than a hundred years passed before the U.S. Senate passed a bill outlawing the intrastate murder of civil rights workers, and then it did so over the solid vote of Southern Senators from states which refuse to indict the accused murderers under their own laws.

The American struggle for civil rights legislation was frustrated for years by Senate Rule 22—the "liberum veto" of the filibuster. Rule 22, requiring the affirmative vote of two-thirds of the present-and-voting Senators before debate can be cut off and the roll called, enables a small group of determined opponents to kill an act supported by the majority by simply preventing it from coming to a vote. In 1968 a filibuster prevented the confirmation of President Johnson's nomination of Abe Fortas as Chief Justice of the Supreme Court. Although that filibuster was clearly partisan, its success proved to have been a disguised blessing when Justice Fortas, involved in a conflict-of-interest scandal a few months later, was forced to resign. The history of the filibuster presents a sort of ideological smorgasbord. Twenty years before Fortas a principled stand by one man, Senator Robert Taft, prevented the conscription of striking railroad workers, and thirty years before that another principled filibuster by a mere half-dozen Senators kept the United States out of the League of Nations.

Why doesn't the absolute liberty of the filibuster bring The State down? In theory, it does. In practice, it is broken (as it was in the passage of the civil rights legislation of the 1960's) by the application of the central principle being argued here: Whenever a big enough majority wants badly enough to do anything, it does it. The pressure of the electorate, the federal executive, and the federal courts for desegregation became irresistible, and so the proponents of the majority view, when the opposition rose in the Senate to exercise liber-

133

ty in the form of the "right of unlimited debate," were at last ready to talk that liberty to death.

There are three *subsocietal* institutions which in theory preserve the uncoerced rights of every member—but none of them is the "team" which Prime Minister Macmillan analogized. The connotation of team as a group (of animals or men) pulling together and remaining united without somehow sacrificing individual liberties is a happy one. Men like to think of an ideal society, and even of a more limited operating organization, in this way. But the eleven men in the football huddle are no more a team, in any permanent, continuing sense, than is a Congress or a Parliament debating the national budget. At some point action has got to be taken, and at that point freedom of discussion ends. The referee, stop-watch in hand, blows the whistle for play and the quarterback says to his team-mates: "Here's what we'll do. . . ."

Apart from the short-lived "utopias," with their overt or implied religious motivation, there are a few (very few) small religious sects which proceed on the basis of absolute liberty and, therefore, of absolute unanimity. The best known is the Religious Society of Friends (Quakers), which, without stated dogma or ordained ministry, conducts even its business affairs in the religious spirit of pure democracy. The Quakers hold that since "there is that of God in every man," no man's will may be violated by men—be they a majority, a minority, a priest or a pope. No man may represent—and, possibly, misrepresent—any other. When the local meeting of Friends assembles, not for worship, but for business, no decision may be taken if as few as one Friend is "uneasy," or undecided.

This principle, obviously impossible of application to

the community, the state, or the nation, is, at bottom, also traditional to the concept of the family. In theory (and in fact in primitive cultures) family sovereignty may be undivided, the husband ("Mister" or "Master" to his wife) exacting the fulfillment of the wife's promise to love, honor and *obey;* but in all societies (and much more so under modern social conditions) the wife has a "veto," however guilefully she may exercise it, and, upon close analysis, so do the children. Family decisions—including even the husband's choice of occupation—are taken at least with the "advice and *consent*" of the wife; and as the children develop toward maturation, they play an ever increasing role in the family's governance. The small boy whose mother coerces him to brush his teeth may demur on this point, or the hen-pecked husband, or the rooster-pecked wife; but the principle of unanimity is nevertheless operative, both in modern domestic theory and to an increasing degree in modern domestic practice.

The advantage of free unanimity is obvious: The organization which acts only with the express approval of every one of its members, and only when dissent is overcome by honest convincement, is a power house. The truly united family has the strength that the great society hasn't; the ambition of the free nation's president to achieve "consensus" (like the ambition of the tyrant to achieve *Einheit* or unity) looks to a degree of effectiveness which even a free society cannot achieve if it is sizable. Thus it is that a small sect like the Quakers—with perhaps 125,000 members in the whole world—is so well known around the globe for its social action programs. Nothing is harder to stop than a freely and fully united band of human beings.

But the family, like the Quaker Meeting, need not

"work." First, it is not usually called upon to function decisively at any given temporal point. There are, of course, emergencies in any family, but these are not the norm, nor the determinant in family relations. Domestic or congregational decisions ordinarily can be debated for weeks or months, or even years. But The State must act, and act every day, on a thousand-and-one fronts or perish. Distant matters it may postpone for a time; but immediate matters require the innumerable immediate decisions of government at every level. Second, it is not necessarily fatal to those involved if the family and the sect do not "work" at all: the veto, arbitrarily exercised, means divorce in one case and dissolution in the other; and after it is over the world and its nation-States go on. The relationship among individuals involved in the family and the sect, even though its potentiality is natural to them, is an artifact in the sense that it is an arrangement freely entered into and freely (if sometimes painfully) dissoluble; as that of man and The State is not. He who would divorce himself from The State finds it fearfully difficult to do so; if, for example, he objects to its taxes, or its wars, or its interference with his Saturday night bath when the town is on fire. And if he succeeds in dissolving the union, as most men cannot hope to do, where will he go but to another State whose denial of his individual sovereignty is identical, in principle, with the one he left?

Let individuals divorce, or the congregation dissolve, and the members go their way without, necessarily, ever coming into further contact or conflict with one another. The citizen is in no such situation; he cannot walk out and never see The State again. Neither can all the citizens (or some of them, by revolution) dissolve The

State without proceeding to organize another. Nor can the sovereign nation-States of the world divorce one another, that is, "break off relations," without inducing a train of tremendous consequences including, sooner or later, war. The law and custom that hold The State (and the community of nation-States) together are human and as fragile as all human bonds, while the bonds of the family and the religious sect are those of love and of God, which are less susceptible to rupture. I once heard of a devout Christian (whose wife was a notorious trial to him) who said to a friend: "If it were not for the canons of the Church I'd have taken a meat axe to her on a hundred occasions." The canons of The State are not so successful.

The third subsocietal institution in which the liberty of the individual is supreme is the closest to our concern here because, like The State, it is secular, and, indeed, an organ of The State. This is the trial jury, every one of whose twelve members must agree on a verdict. This most singular of public bodies is constituted to give the accused (in a criminal case) the benefit of the doubt, and the requirement of unanimity is intended to enhance that benefit: better that ten guilty go free than that one innocent be convicted.

But jury membership, too, like that of the family and the sect, is free and dissoluble. A venireman may be excused—in practice, excuse himself—if he cannot on his own affirmation accept the burden of the jury, say, to inflict capital punishment (or even to send a man to prison). And the "hung jury," which cannot reach a decision, may be dismissed and the case retried.

The *liberum veto* of the one "holdout" juror, exercising absolute liberty, may then "hang" the jury (and force a retrial) or even, if his fellow-jurors despair of

137

bringing him over to their view, result in an actual reversal of the majority position. What are the consequences of this untrammeled liberty which, in the conduct of The State as a whole, would be anarchy? The worst foreseeable consequence is that a guilty man will be acquitted and returned to society, perhaps to continue his depredations. In the ordinary course such acquittal constitutes no clear and present danger to society's survival, or to the maintenance of law and order. One more criminal is at large. Society endures the jeopardy rather than abolish the unanimity safeguard of the rights of the accused.

The trial juror is a truly phenomenal figure in that he, and he alone, as juror enjoys inalienable rights; greater, incidentally, than a Supreme Court justice, who cannot prevent a verdict of the Court but can only record his dissent and bow to majority rule. The juror—the single juror—is sovereign, and sovereignty is power. And power unchecked is dangerous. Just as one of the great powers interested in Poland's destruction had only to corrupt one sovereign member of the *sejm,* so a defendant in a jury case has to "reach" only one member of the jury to escape conviction. And however circumspectly the jurors may be isolated during their service, there are a dozen ways of getting to one of them (even before they are formally impaneled). So commonplace is jury tampering that in 1967 England replaced the unanimous verdict with the requirement of agreement by ten of the twelve jurors; it is harder to corrupt three jurors than one. (During the Parliamentary debate, an opponent of the measure, protesting that the unanimous verdict had been an English law for six hundred years, was reminded that the Scots had had the majority verdict for a thousand.)

In practice, of course, the situation of the honest juror is far from uninhibited, just as it is in the family and the congregation. The "holdout" juror is under the greatest pressure from his fellow-jurors: studies of the jury system all support the supposition that one or two of the twelve, standing alone, tend to yield, if not to the arguments, to the *weight* of the ten or eleven (and the plea to agree so that they can all be discharged and go home). So, too, the husband probably dominates the wife (at least on a percentage basis). And the "uneasy" Quaker may grow uneasier still under the burden of hamstringing action, especially when the strong advocates of action are "weighty Friends." So even in these three bodies, whose members are uniquely endowed with freedom of action, liberty yields to authority more often than not.

On even the happiest reading of their experience, the three truly free types of human relationship are too far from the experience of man with The State to suggest a resolution of the great dilemma. There is, and can be, no sovereign State which does not at some point sacrifice the individual to the real or imagined general welfare. The beating-a-dead-horse complaint remains: "What of it? Don't we rock along pretty well? Haven't the centuries, and especially the last few, shown progress in our political institutions?" The issue of progress may be debated, but not at this level. In respect to the essential relationship of man and The State, we are precisely where we were a century ago when Abraham Lincoln, in his first message to Congress, asked, "Must a government of necessity be too *strong* for the liberties of its own people, or too *weak* to maintain its own existence?" And where Lincoln was in 1860 (and Socrates twenty-two centuries earlier) mankind always has been.

Our reader may then say, "So we don't rock along pretty well, and there is no progress—still, what of it? You don't argue with necessity, with breath or with death. You accept the insolubility of the problem and make the best of it and keep pushing for individual liberty as hard as you can." But why for liberty? Why not for authority? Why for the individual, and not for The State? And here, I think, the case is clinched. Men all proclaim liberty, fight for it, and even die for it, because they believe that The State is the inherent enemy of liberty; that "eternal vigilance" which Jefferson termed the price of liberty was vigilance against The State. Men do not believe that The State needs to be stronger, unless they are frightened of still stronger enemies from without or within. The reasoned argument for the stronger State—like that of *The Federalist*—is based squarely on the stronger State's increased capacity to preserve and advance the liberties of the citizen.

There may be those who have no qualms about the headlong increase of The State's power, spurred by technology and its consequent centralization, by war and the threat of war, and by the demand for social justice through the medium of "welfare." Individuals and factions to whom these developments are immediately advantageous are not likely to be hesitant to accept them. But the State power waxes, be it well or badly used. And the most thoughtful of those who concede the inevitability of that historical process are disturbed by what they take to be its inevitable concomitant, the reduction of the liberties of the individual by law and of the individual himself by custom and conformity proceeding from the same causes.

The conscious consideration of the issue raised here

may, in addition, have certain specific implications for the conduct of the national life. The irreconcilable divergence in the highest decisions of their country's highest court has often been cited as an occasion of failing faith on the part of the American people in their institutions. Cynicism is certainly born of the insistence of a body like the Nuremberg Tribunal that a soldier may be hanged for obeying his officer. Disenchantment certainly follows the fact that the American and Soviet supporters of opposing sides in a war like Korea's or Vietnam's are equally entitled to fly the U.N. flag. And despair cannot but be the consequence of the successive failure of "world organizations" to fulfill their splendid promises, and the callous disregard of their "peace-keeping machinery" by the unilateral action of the great powers or alliances when they do not trust the organization to act to their advantage.

We speak easily of "the free world" and "the slave world," but in the absence of any clear definition of liberty the totalitarian "people's republics" and "democratic republics" are equally entitled with the nations of "the free world" to claim, as they do, that *they* have true liberty and what *we* have is in fact the tyranny of private profit. So, too, the debate on world government and world federalism goes on from generation to generation without any resolution of the question of such a system's proper powers or the individual's relationship to them. Most Americans doubtless know that there is a World Court at The Hague; what they don't know is why it is called a court and under what conditions a nation is brought into court. Their confusion is well grounded. Nations go to The Hague voluntarily or not at all. The Connolly Act forbids the United States to be a party to a case in the World Court without the express consent of Congress. The other great powers have less explicit but equally binding reservations. The Court may settle issues which two contending nations are willing to have it settle, such small issues as damages in the accidental sinking of a ship of one flag by the ship of another. But let the issue be vital to one or both of the nations involved, and the "Court" has no power at all to bring them in, judge them, or punish them for disturbing the peace; war may be consuming the world, and the Court still sits in The Hague judging disputes over postal rates, weather signals, or fishing grounds; it is no more a court than the United Nations Organization is an organization. (France and the Soviet Union can refuse to pay a duly levied U.N.O. assessment and not lose their membership.)

The immediate issue is not whether the problem of liberty and authority is soluble. Nor is it whether we are condemned to go on crying, "Liberty," without knowing what we are crying. The immediate issue is whether we have any ground for asserting the problem's solubility (or insolubility) without consciously confronting the problem; the question is whether we are manipulating it for purposes of propaganda, deceit, and self-deceit.

The individual, if he is asked which he will choose, if choose he must, tyranny or anarchy, will probably reply as Socrates did when he was asked whether he would rather injure or be injured: "Rather neither." Anarchy—the absolute liberty of the individual—is outside his experience and his comprehension. The overnight anarchy (or liberty) of a Thoreau has no more reality than the life of the hermit who accepts a letter with The State's postage stamp on it.

Let Lenin, of all people, say, "While the State exists,

there is no freedom. When there is freedom, there will be no state." The fact is that anarchy, if it is not that of the freak, but the condition of a whole people, is nothing more nor less than those few days or hours of transition from one social form to another (or back to the same one). It is revolution while the old regime is falling and the new one is not yet established; and the willful breaking of a law, any law, just or unjust, is revolution in principle. Whoever chooses anarchy, and thinks he does so philosophically because he cannot abide the alternative of totalitarianism offered him by the dialectic, is making his choice temperamentally, and not philosophically at all. He is simply gifted (or cursed) with the classic disposition of Mr. Jones of Johnstown, Pa., whose family, perched on the roof of the house to escape the flood, pondered his derby floating back and forth along the length of the property in front of the house; until Mrs. Jones recalled that her husband had said the night before that he was going to mow the lawn the next day come hell or high water.

EPILOGUE:

The Voices of the Young

MILTON MAYER *presented an early version of* Man v. The State *to the Fellows of the Center for the Study of Democratic Institutions in 1965. His ideas since have been refined by first-hand experience with the manner in which the rush of contemporary events raise in new perspective the ancient issues of freedom and authority. On his home grounds he has been active in the opposition to United States involvement in Vietnam. And in the course of regular residence abroad he made protracted visits to Czechoslovakia before and after the Communist regime's "January Spring" of liberalization and the "August Winter" of Russian occupation.*

Mr. Mayer's study of the Czech resistance was published as a Center Occasional Paper, The Art of the Impossible, *in April 1969.* Man v. The State *will appear in a collection of his essays to be published in 1970 by Atheneum. In October, 1969, his central thesis again was the subject of dialogue at the Center, this time with the primary focus on the views of the generation now caught up in what some of its leaders call a youth revolution.*

Three Junior Fellows of the Center prepared written commentaries:

RICHARD J. PARKER, *who majored in philosophy at Dartmouth and has been active in the youth movement in New York, Alabama, and elsewhere;* SUSAN ROSENBLUM, *a graduate of Washington University with a special interest in the communitarian movement; and* MARC A. TRIEBWASSER, *Lehman Fellow in politics at New York University, and an activist in the radical Jewish youth movement. Also participating in the discussion were* STEVEN J. BARTLETT, *who is completing work on a doctorate in the philosophy of science at the University of Paris, and* PIERS VON SIMSON, *a graduate of Oxford, and of the Law School of the University of California at Berkeley.*

Senior Fellows of the Center who took part in the dialogue were HARRY S. ASHMORE, ELISABETH MANN BORGESE, REXFORD G. TUGWELL, HARVEY WHEELER *and* JOHN WILKINSON; *they were joined by* CLIFTON FADIMAN, *editorial consultant to the Center, and* STANLEY SHEINBAUM, *an Associate.*

PARKER: Mr. Mayer tells us that "in the middle of the twentieth century the revolution is *against* the rule of law, now identified as the *enemy* of liberty." He is in search of "the basis, if there is one to be found, upon which the citizen may be protected against The State, or the individual against society, without the danger of anarchy and the ruin of the community." He honestly warns us that "the problem may be insoluble." But he also tells us that "it does not follow that it is a dead horse that will bear no further beating." I suspect he is wrong. He has given us an admirable survey of the poor beast's carcass, but no means of raising it from the dead.

My first major objection to Mr. Mayer's approach is systemic. Despite asseverations to the contrary, I think a good deal of his argument rests on a continuum between individual liberty and state authority: if one goes up, the other must go down. The notion certainly has famous antecedents, but it can be misleading. Mr. Mayer concedes this when he admits the difficulty of recognizing what our freedoms are: are they those of the Bill of Rights, or do they also include freedom from building codes, freedom from community moral standards, and freedom from dress codes? Most of us would agree that repression of the freedom of speech is part of the continuum; but when the Federal Government limits one-bank holding companies, or specifies the amount of chicken in our hot dogs, I wonder how many of us think of these issues in terms of freedom, or even think of them at all. In warning us that "the immediate issue is whether we have any ground for asserting the problem's solubility . . . without consciously confronting its *reality*," Mr. Mayer has opened Pandora's box. The *reality* of freedom is an abyss from which one never escapes. Mr. Mayer's only salvation is in sticking primarily to Constitution-related examples.

My second objection is also systemic, and follows from the first. In employing his liberty-authority continuum, Mr. Mayer utilizes a polarity that, to my mind, unjustifiably gives a sense of equal weight to the probability of anarchy and totalitarianism when the imagined mean between them is violated. In no sense do I concede that anarchy and repression are equally likely consequences of social disobedience; the latter clearly outclasses its opponent. If and when anarchy (or more properly, the overthrow of the present government and its replacement with another) comes about, given the present means of repression, it will involve the majority of the populace, or damn near the majority, and thereby meet everyone's definition of acceptable revolution. Obedience is so much a characteristic of contemporary social life, from childhood on, I find it impossible to imagine that at any one time the probability of anarchy could be equivalent to that of tyranny.

My third objection is not to the answers Mr. Mayer gives, but to the question he asks. I simply am not interested in his concern with liberty *in vitro*, rather than *in vivo*. The abolition of polygamy may limit my freedom, but I don't really care—other things worry me more. Like Mr. Mayer, "if I only had a standing rule to go by . . . I should know what moved me to do what." But the rule hasn't been discovered, and doesn't seem on the verge of being discovered, and I must go on.

Unlike Mr. Mayer, I really don't think that "to rest on the proposition that the central problem of political life . . . is insoluble is to accept the counsel of despair," any more than I think it was despair that drove scientists to stop asking how the universe started, or philosophers to abandon their inquiry into the nature of the soul. There just seem to be a lot more important, and potentially soluble, problems right under our noses. Mr. Mayer insists that "we dare not consign such an issue to academic limbo;" but maybe a little more time on the shelf gathering still more dust wouldn't really hurt a question of such ancient vintage.

ROSENBLUM: Current rebellions against the rule of law can be seen as rejection of the nation state, and a growing expression of identification with world community and the family of man, associations which at this point in history have no concrete political structure.

Civil rights and anti-war demonstrations, if carried out non-violently, seek to re-affirm what Martin Luther King described as "the beloved community." Those who participate may see themselves as Garrison did: "My country is the world, my countrymen are mankind." Transnational identification and humanitarian outlook motivate such individuals to break civil laws.

It is in this light that we can understand the attraction of Herbert Marcuse's philosophy of "repressive tolerance," a plea for society to base its laws on explicit value commitments to a more humanistic civilization. Marcuse argues for a concept of liberty and freedom which tolerates all enterprises which are nonviolent, liberating, progressive and humanistic, but would allow us to repress (or not tolerate) actions which tend to be reactionary, violent, and explicitly antihumanistic. Marcuse believes that "toleration" cannot be indiscriminate, but must "tolerate movements from the Left and intolerate or repress movements from the Right."

Mr. Mayer properly reminds us that this does not settle the question of who in society is going to decide what is progressive and what is reactionary. Nevertheless, Marcuse's doctrine demands serious consideration as our society becomes more technological and self-destructive. The pollution of the environment; the biological revolution which raises the possibility of man's controlling the nature and longevity of his own species; and, above all, the suffering and struggle of Third World peoples to liberate themselves from violent colonial situations, *demand* that we re-think the meaning of such traditional concepts as individual liberty, authority, and even democracy. The revolution in cybernetics, transportation, and communication is rapidly making the concept of The State obsolete.

As members of a world community, and not merely citizens of a national state, we will require a new legal code. Its purpose could be to maximize the quality of human life rather than the preservation of law and order. The changing relationship of man to the environment also will demand new interpretations of "individual liberty" and "security." When we begin to think of The Community as the locus of human association rather than The State, the problem will be seen as that of the individual seeking self-fulfillment while contributing to the growth of the group. The maintenance of individual liberty thus changes context, and priority.

The issues posed by *Man v. The State* ought to be restated to deal primarily with man's relationship to the world and his environment. The resurgence of communal movements is a conscious attempt to re-examine basic philosophical questions, and to find alternatives (through human organizations) to the alienation of modern society. Concepts such as The State and individual liberty are the product of the Industrial Revolution; now in the post-industrial era we are oppressing other peoples and killing ourselves, making senseless wars and polluting the natural environment, to keep sacred these shibboleths. A poster in a Berkeley bookstore suggests the need for a new manifesto: "A Declaration of Interdependence . . ."

TRIEBWASSER: Since I do not believe that liberalism supplies an adequate formulation for meeting human needs, and therefore am not a liberal, I am not as concerned as Mr. Mayer with the absolute protection of individual freedom. I have a paramount need for belonging, and I believe most people do. The cult of the individual in America has neglected this very human drive, and this is one of the reasons for the widespread feelings of alienation in my generation.

But, while I am willing to give up some aspects of my freedom in the name of group participation, I am willing to do so only if I feel I am able to function fully in the determination of the group's policies. Social organizations which are thus able to fulfill my human needs (not guarantee my absolute liberty, which I really do not want anyway) must be of such a nature, and of such a size, as to allow for effective participation by every member. It is not a matter of adamantly refusing to give up some aspects of one's individuality; but of refusal to yield individuality to social institutions which fail to meet human needs.

Mr. Mayer seems to be seeking a universal solution for the problems of political and social institutions. Perhaps if we recognize that there can be no universal social code we will see that men can organize good societies in various ways. Then we might allow for, and actively encourage the development of communities based on different principles of social organization, thus giving the individual the choice of a variety of communities he might like to join. I argue for pluralism, and you cannot have pluralism and universality at the same time.

MAYER: Although the Junior Fellows seem to disagree with one another, they seem to agree that my argument is not relevant to the problems of the day. What I am trying to say is this: that to talk about *limited* or responsible government is to talk about government which does not have the power it may need to preserve The State. Consider, for example, these items culled from the newspapers of the last few days:

The Secretary of State, Mr. William Rogers, says: "When it is clear that the American people support President Nixon in the Vietnam policy that he has established and is carrying out, then I think it is possible the enemy will negotiate a settlement. At the moment I think this is quite unlikely because there is so much dissent here." Other members of the Administration have been more explicit, arguing that dissent on Vietnam is treason, and that we can't do anything about ending the war because of some people's perverse refusal to close ranks behind the President.

Then there is the report of a strike by the Montreal

police in which a provincial policeman was killed, and four persons were wounded. Banks have been held up, and arson, rioting and looting were widespread over a twenty-four hour period. There was anarchy in Montreal, and the alternative to anarchy in Montreal is slavery.

The Montreal policeman is Officer Sweeney in my paper: he's a man with a wife and 17 children, and his salary is not high enough to make ends meet, and he has said, I'm not going to live like this any longer, I quit! But some Canadian Calvin Coolidge has said to him, oh, no, you're not going to quit; you can't strike against the public, which means against The State. If the policeman agrees, he is saying, I'm a slave, and indeed he is. If Officer Sweeney says, as he did last week in Montreal, I'm not a slave, he has plunged society into a hopelessly anarchic situation.

ASHMORE: Mr. Parker complained that you have established a continuum that runs from anarchy to slavery, and you seem to be bearing him out.

MAYER: There's a line in Thoreau which I don't think appears in this document of mine, although almost every line everybody else has written on the subject does. Thoreau said that it ought to be possible for a man to live within the geographical area of The State and neither be a burden on it, nor have it be a burden on him. As recently as 100 years ago, when J. Edgar Hoover first took office, you could imagine people living in cracks and crevices of the civilization, neither taking from The State nor giving to it. I don't know whether this was good or bad; but I can see the possibility that it was so.

ASHMORE: Are you then contending that any duty or obligation The State may impose is a burden?

MAYER: Yes, when society requires that I accept a burden and leaves me no way to walk out of society, then I'm a slave.

ASHMORE: There are no obligations or duties that you would recognize?

MAYER: Oh, there are obligations that are upon me—I wouldn't say as a citizen—but as a child of God. There are obligations that are upon me. . . .

ASHMORE: I'm talking only about those transmitted through government—obligations to The State, duties required by it, imposed by it, owed to it . . . Is there *any* obligation you must assume to The State you live under that is not a burden and therefore does not reduce you to slavery?

MAYER: No, I would say none.

WHEELER: Why don't you refine your idea of slavery so we can get out of some of these terminological problems? We have had chattel slavery, and wage slavery, and now the soldier is confronted with a special kind of political slavery—the result of the polity as a whole deciding that those bearing certain random numbers shall be put to work killing people. What you are talking about apparently is something that might better be called functional slavery. The governmental situation now is such that many options are foreclosed to people, often without their agreement. This isn't technical slavery in the ordinary sense, but it creates restrictions its victims can do nothing about.

MAYER: It might be possible to make a set of objective distinctions in connection with the term slavery. I'm not sure, however, that you can make subjective distinctions, and these may be what count. You may say to a conscripted soldier that he is not a chattel slave as Negroes were before the Civil War, or a wage slave as his father was before the unions freed him, and he may reply that he doesn't see that it makes any difference—he still has lost his freedom and is being forced to do work he abhors.

WHEELER: Your point then is that the situation we are in today is such that increasing categories of people have a subjective feeling of slavery, and this feeling is the determinant, whether or not it is theoretically justified?

MAYER: Yes, a growing number have increasingly intense feelings of subjection to slavery, with, let me add, good reason.

WHEELER: The conclusion that follows is that there's no way out. You are saying the controversies cannot be resolved?

MAYER: The minute I try to see a way out, I have destroyed The State. When we talk about subjective destruction we are talking about anarchy.

WHEELER: But a constitutionalist like Rex Tugwell can come back at you and say, what do you mean, anarchy? This dispute between workers and The State is just another problem to be resolved; maybe we don't have adequate arbitration machinery, but we can do better in the future. It does not follow that we face the choice between slavery and anarchy because some policemen, or garbage collectors, or soldiers are denied the right to strike.

MAYER: We are all compelled to share what I regard as Mr. Tugwell's innocence. If we don't share it, the problem is indeed insoluble on any level and there's nothing left to talk about; we must hope that somehow the system can be made to work better. But here I am—I belong to an association, the association has a contract, neither party has broken it but the contract has expired, and the question is: what hours, wages and working conditions am I going to have if I continue to collect garbage after January 1? The State offers me what I consider a slave wage, and that's subjective slavery, at least. So I say, no, under those conditions I'm not going to collect garbage. And at this point, you know what The State will do . . . compel me to collect garbage on penalty of going to jail.

TRIEBWASSER: Your mistake is in treating the problem as purely political and not taking into account the social and economic factors. You make it sound as though one's liberty is only impinged upon by government. The question has been put in the matrix of the individual versus the totality. We should be thinking of social sub-groups which may deal with man's responsibility to other men without directly involving The State. The State should be very minimally involved in our communities, and allow each to evolve its own structure—recognizing that it doesn't matter that community A is different from community B. We should be looking for good *societies* instead of looking for *the* good society. If we had various communes with different ideals, truly different ideals, then one could pull out of one commune and find his way into another which might satisfy him more.

MAYER: The difficulty is that your communes would still exist in a world, a cosmos, made up of governments, with the equivalent of laws of nature like gravity. You can "do what you want"—provided you pay taxes and what not; you don't argue with gravity. Within this cosmos there may be "free" groups, "free" communes, living any way they want—but only so long as they pay their taxes, go to war, get their vaccinations, go to school, marry one woman at a time, etc., for those are requirements of the laws of nature.

TRIEBWASSER: But all those things do not have to be relegated to The State. Because of our fixation with western European political concepts, I don't think we appreciate the possibilities of pluralistic societies. I don't think we understand, for example, the fact that in the Moslem world there were various principalities living very close to each other with vastly different laws, and ways were found of working these things out. This was also true of the early European folk societies. I think we can limit The State much further than we have, while at the same time we deal with social organizations through community control, through communes, or other structures of participatory democracy.

MAYER: Here is the only man in the house who's got anything that I can see as workable—or would be if only technology hadn't got going, if only J. Edgar Hoover and Samuel F. B. Morse hadn't been born.

TRIEBWASSER: I think the pluralism I'm talking about is possible because of the technology. The computers can be used, for example, to help people with similar interest and life styles get together.

FADIMAN: The essential point of this whole argument has now been reached. The question is whether within a technological society you can have what are in essence tribal structures. Examples from Moslem culture, or from early European culture, involve certain assumptions: to wit, the existence of a sparse and very poor population. When you try to institute tribal cultures within an enormous technological web, the connections of the web will sooner or later reach out into the little struggling tribes or communes and begin to destroy them. Within the web of a technological society, is it possible to institute pluralism—to go back, as I see it, about 10,000 years?

WHEELER: This is the question all right. Mr. Mayer is not avoiding it when he starts with a proposition that rests upon certain distinctions in classical liberal theory about the relationship between liberty and The State. He goes on to contend that this way of looking at these relationships is wrong, and no longer of any use. What Kafka said in *The Trial* and in *The Castle,* is now true of every political entity in the modern world, at least in the advanced world. This means it is futile to follow the old liberal rules, it doesn't do you any good. I take it that Mr. Mayer is asking for an entirely new body of political theory—a theory of The State which might allow for some degree of re-tribalization and autonomy so that if people can't revolt, at least they can follow John Locke's prescription and go some place else until they find the kind of slavery they happen to enjoy under a concept of The State that supports such a choice. Am I anywhere near your meaning, when I say that what we need is a new doctrine of The State?

MAYER: Fair enough. But let me note that where I find Mill and the rest crossing themselves up, I think they will still be crossed up when we produce your new doctrine of The State. I think this issue is insoluble on the theoretical level. Can you figure out a constitution under which man can live in the way prescribed by that line of Thoreau's I quoted? He must have something to do with The State, and The State may have something to do with him, but one need not crush the other. This is the issue. I am waiting for someone to outline an organization of society in which I can still escape—an organization that fits not a pastoral culture but an advanced technological society, because that's where we've all got to live.

WILKINSON: Nobody has suggested how one could overcome the deficiencies and perils of a technological society. We burble on about man still being free, when it is clear that he is not—not free, at least, of the technological imperatives. Mr. Fadiman was certainly right in putting his finger on this as the key issue. But it does not follow that the slave versus free man distinction is unimportant.

FADIMAN: It's unimportant because in time the technological society will condition all citizens so that they will have rid themselves of the illusion of freedom. It will take us to a *brave new world.*

ROSENBLUM: Isn't the question whether we haven't failed in our efforts to reorganize society institutionally? When the young talk about communes and the idea of community they describe an experience in human relations which does not have to be institutionalized or structured too formally. Perhaps it's not possible to seek this experience by creating new institutions, or by working formally within the old ones; it's a much more subjective experience people are looking for today. The concept of individual liberty is giving way to the concept of individual self-fulfillment, and while the two are related, the second is less concerned with political freedom and more with psychological and personal freedom. It's hard to find ways to institutionalize the *feeling* of community. What we are moving toward is a revolution in human relationships . . .

WHEELER: I think that's a good lead for Mr. Mayer, too. We can only follow this line on the level of subjectivity. The young people are talking about a new pluralism that doesn't rest upon the kinds of formal structures that have been associated with classical pluralistic doctrine in the past, but rather rests upon individual perception.

MAYER: What these young people are saying is undoubtedly important. This is what the revolution is about, the one that's going on in the United States, the one that's going on everywhere else in the world, with the greatest intensity in the advanced countries. The young cannot, they will not, accept the imperative with which this document of mine confronts them. They will not accept the condition with which it leaves them. So they must find a new way to live. They say they're going to live differently, as if somehow The State were not there. But this raises certain difficulties. For example, in order to enlist in the experiential revolution, the first thing you've got to do if you're male and between 18 and 26 is find a way to freak out of the draft.

WHEELER: Those who are still on the same wave length seem to be talking about what might be called a new individualism. It's obviously not anything like the old individualism because that was the foundation of the system the young people abhor. What is this new individualism?

PARKER: I'm not sure it would be defined as individualism, because individualism slips back in again to that atomic model that Mr. Mayer still uses, and it keeps screwing us up, every time we come back to it. I think most of my generation has been thoroughly conditioned by Freud in the concept of the history of civilization as a history of repression. We concede that certain measures of repression are necessary and that we're not going to escape from them, and so we don't even take up the problem that concerns Mr. Mayer. What we're concerned with is the way Marcuse looks at society when he asks are there conditions of *surplus* repression—repression that is not necessary for our functioning as selves in our community? We're most interested in the gap between what we have and the least amount of repression and oppression we can exist with.

MAYER: This may be a bogus dichotomy, but I would

like to find out how at one and the same time you do your thing and live in a commune.

ROSENBLUM: I've had some experience living in a nonviolent community in Pennsylvania. It included a group of high school and college students who were strongly politically oriented toward social change. There also was a group of young people who were very much interested in art and sensitivity experience, who saw the real revolution as an individual and experiential process. There was a great deal of conflict the summer I lived in the community. The art group people kept going off during the work hour and playing the guitar instead of helping out with the community chores. At the same time the political people were out demonstrating and leafleting in town when they were supposed to be at the farm. The community didn't work because some were not willing to do as Marc suggests—weigh the advantages of what you give up to balance what you receive. The idea of doing your own thing is not the purpose of living in community. It's a mistake to think that community is something that just spontaneously comes about; it has to be created through the experience of sharing. It requires effort and cooperation.

MAYER: Effort, and a sacrifice of individual liberty?

ROSENBLUM: Community requires the exercise of self-discipline.

TUGWELL: You're talking about organization now. There has to be organization?

ROSENBLUM: The intentional community, if it is going

to be relevant to the outside world, have a purpose and hold together, does require some kind of structure. But in addition to structure, "community" also describes an experience in human relationship. A very strong emotional bond emerges among the people who participate and build the community.

ASHMORE: How big was your community?

ROSENBLUM: Throughout the summer there was a core group of about 35 to 40.

ASHMORE: Was your purpose to be self-sufficient?

ROSENBLUM: No, the purpose of the community was to give human relations training and to motivate young people to become change agents, so that they would be able to go back to their schools and communities and work for nonviolent social change.

TUGWELL: I take it from what you said that the difficulty was a lack of discipline?

ROSENBLUM: I would say lack of understanding among the young people as to the meaning of "community."

TUGWELL: Which would have produced self-discipline?

ROSENBLUM: Yes. Community does require self-discipline—it is not simply a place to come and do your own thing.

MAYER: And in the absence of self-discipline, and in the absence of external discipline, the community broke up? Either one would have kept it together, self-discipline or external discipline—a police force, and so on, possibly a touch of dictatorship. But what you had was a communion, I would guess, and this wound up in dissolution—something that is not allowed to happen to, say, the United States or the Soviet Union.

ASHMORE: My ancestors in South Carolina gave it a pretty good try.

MAYER: That's so, and it took four years of fraternal persuasion. . . .

ASHMORE: I think we would have called it coercion.

MAYER: Anyway, there was nothing like that in Miss Rosenblum's community. One fellow goes off, playing his guitar, another goes off distributing leaflets, and no one is left to do the work required by the general welfare and the communal good. Now, Mr. Triebwasser, you have heard this testimony that you don't enter the commune for the purpose of doing your thing, nor does the commune guarantee you the unrestricted right to do your thing. This was what you were talking about when you said you didn't want all this liberty?

TRIEBWASSER: When you put it in terms of doing your thing you miss the heart of the matter. The controlling factor is self-fulfillment: one of the needs, one of the requirements of self-fulfillment is belonging. Fulfillment may require one to accept limits on some aspects of one's activity in order to keep the community together, but the very limitation may be part of fulfilling oneself. It is a two-way relationship between individual and community. Doing your own thing is not, it is a carry-on of the cult of the individual.

ROSENBLUM: Doing your own thing is the antithesis of community, I think.

MAYER: Isn't doing your own thing the end, the ultimate of all of these operations?

TRIEBWASSER: No, it's self-fulfillment.

MAYER: OK, let's do away with doing your own thing. Self-fulfillment, then, is the living end.

ROSENBLUM: There is something about the experience of living in communities that is essential if we are going to resocialize people. Communal life has a unique ability to change people's outlooks and values, and at this stage in society it is more educational than political or revolutionary. This experience must come before we can think about transforming a total society into a community, or doing away with The State. . . .

MAYER: Yes, but meanwhile all of you are in The State, and the course you are advocating leads me to suggest that you are, shall I say, playing house. It's a form of escapism. We all try to escape, one way or another.

TRIEBWASSER: We are not escaping from a human society. . . .

MAYER: No, you are not escaping. You are indulging in escapism, but not escaping. Look, in order to have the kind of community, the pluralistic society, the tribes and so on that you have been talking about, you still have to beat the conscription agents if you're between 18 and 26. Try that for a starter.

TRIEBWASSER: But the point is not simply to go off into the woods and form a community. The point is to change the structure of society so as to foster human values. The matter on my mind isn't simply one, if you will, of individual salvation. The question becomes one of group salvation, and using the group to try to change things. This isn't simply escapism.

MAYER: Group salvation. At the sacrifice of the individual? Or never quite that?

TRIEBWASSER: I am looking for a society in which I can achieve self-fulfillment. At the same time, I recognize that in order for me to have that sort of society, it must provide self-fulfillment for other people. I realize that I must be awfully careful about other people's ability to fulfill themselves; therefore, there is a question of balance. It is a responsibility for the individual, but not only for myself. In political terms, I concede that in order to preserve my own liberty I must be very careful to try to preserve other people's liberty.

TUGWELL: We used to call that being a good citizen.

ROSENBLUM: A redefinition of politics seems to be under way in the youth movement. Back in 1962 when Students for a Democratic Society was organized the Port Huron statement was issued, and it went something like this: The purpose of politics is to create an acceptable pattern of social relationships and bring the individual out of isolation and into community. That seems to me a very explicit statement of what community aims to do. Many of the intentional communities in the United States today are very much interested in social change, and see their way of life not only as a means to an end, but an end in itself. They are willing to struggle, and it's the experience of struggle which creates community. They are trying to bring people out of isolation, out of the alienation they feel toward their culture. But we'd like to see it done without violence, or with a minimum of human cost.

WHEELER: There's a great deal of historical evidence available about previous communes, and some of the most interesting concerns the Puritan communities. They existed in two phases: they split off from the English parent bodies first and went to the Low Countries, and then they split again, some returning to England and some coming on to America. One of the conclusions scholars have reached in studying these communities is that the ones that had enough energy to leave England were the ones that had the tightest organization. A tight organization usually meant the dominance of a charismatic leader who didn't hesitate to use his power. Those that disintegrated in the Lowlands were those that did not maintain what can only be called dictatorial organization. And those which survived the second split and made it to the New World were the ones that had the most dictatorial organization of all. This is a fundamental question of the relationship between authority and survival, and it is dominant in the history of all the communitarian efforts. . . .

PARKER: I would say that there would be tight correlation between the concept of obedience inherent in the religion, and the dictatorial structure manifested by the congregations. What I'm trying to suggest is that the concept of a strong-willed obedience is pretty much opposed to the entire *Zeitgeist* of the young right now.

WHEELER: I realize that. That's my reason for bringing it up.

ASHMORE: As an ideal concept, is it conceived that the modern commune becomes self-sufficient? Or would it be, even under optimum conditions, incorporated into the larger community? I've always understood the classic concept to be that of a self-sufficient whole, serving an exemplary role in influencing the community at large toward the good life.

ROSENBLUM: I think the only communities that are going to have a chance at surviving are those which remain open and expect people to enter and leave voluntarily. This would still allow for a humanizing experience when you are a member of that community. Historically, communities have failed when they tried to become self-sufficient, and have cut themselves off so that their members were not involved actively in the life of society.

ASHMORE: Members might live in the community and work outside in the larger world—is that the way you see it too, Marc?

TRIEBWASSER: Well, there are questions as to how things will work out. There is another possibility, com-

167

munes based around functional concepts. If we are in a post-industrial age, then it seems to me that we ought to get rid of some of the drudgery. Human beings can be freed by the machines to do other things, but this may mean reorganizing society in such a way as to split up the drudgery-type jobs that still remain and pass them around part-time among people primarily engaged in doing something else. Maybe it works out that each individual has the responsibility to the community for performing certain fundamental chores, just as a member of the family has to mow the lawn or wash the dishes.

MAYER: These would be assigned chores?

TRIEBWASSER: It would be understood that there are a certain number of things which have to be done, and everybody would have to put a certain amount of time into these communal activities, instead of saying let somebody else do it.

MAYER: But what if everybody in the community wants to do the same thing? There are twenty different things that have to be done. Suppose Mr. Fadiman doesn't want to sit around the table talking, he wants to collect the garbage, but somebody else is already doing it?

TRIEBWASSER: I think your example is poor. There are certain things that no one really wants to do—for example, the dishes have to be washed, the meal has to be cooked, the lawn has to be attended to. . . .

FADIMAN: This is a terribly important point and that's why Mr. Mayer asked you the question. Historically we have a long record of communities in our own land which foundered on precisely that issue and no other. Fruitlands, New Harmony, Brook Farm, I could run through a list of twenty, if you wish. All of them foundered on a trait in human nature which apparently has nothing to do with the form of The State, to wit: A likes to do one thing, B likes to do another. In the case of Fruitlands the trouble was that no one wanted to collect the garbage. They were libertarians, just like you.

TRIEBWASSER: Not like me—I'm not a liberal. I would say very definitely you either do certain of these social functions or. . . .

MAYER: Or you go to another community. You're playing house. Because there's one everlasting community in which you perform certain functions, and if you don't perform them you don't get out of the community, you get shot. That is the Union of Soviet Socialist Republics, and that is the United States of America, and that is every other nation state. I insist you are playing house.

TRIEBWASSER: Will you define what you mean by playing house?

MAYER: Yes sir. Playing house means that if you don't like it, you leave it. You knock the house down the way Susan's friends did last summer. But all the time you are actually living inside, if I may use the phrase, the big house, the real house.

TRIEBWASSER: I say we don't have to have final reliance on The State . . . there may be certain matters of supporting services that would have to be worked out, but then there are certain things life forces us to do in order

169

to get other things done. That is, if you will, a very psychoanalytical approach. . . .

MAYER: But who collects the garbage?

TRIEBWASSER: If you are living in a community you are going to find out that there are certain chores no one likes to do, but they still have to be done. If you don't like to do them then you get out of the relationship, but of course you can't ultimately avoid your share of chores because that's part of living. The problem is not to avoid the chores but to find the community of my choice. If I move to Europe, or to an Asian nation, I am surrounded by the same structures, the same way of handling things. A variety of small communities could offer me an opportunity of moving out of all this and into something else.

MAYER: You'd still be inside the big community.

TRIEBWASSER: We could consider a confederation. I don't like to use these political terms, but the various communities could join for some purposes, like the old city states. You could move around between Verona or Venice or Genoa and there was no big Italy. . . .

MAYER: Now there's One Big Italy, isn't there?

TRIEBWASSER: Breaking up into small communities is not *the* final answer to all human dilemmas. At one point in history the communities were very small, and in order to achieve certain progress they had to centralize. Now we've come to the point where we're over-centralized, and we must decentralize. We may have to centralize again. You are demanding *the* answer, and I say there is no one answer. The reason religions have failed in modern society is that they have been trying to give *the* answer, when there is no such thing. The only thing that is viable in human life is the search for solutions. . . .

MAYER: That's beautiful. I believe it is also called the pursuit of happiness. But you and I, wherever we are, in the United States, Thailand, England, or Russia, are crawling along on our bellies, crushed by the same set of laws. If you don't have *the* answer, what is *one* answer to The State? You told me that The State is the same wherever you are—so I suppose that you're stuck with it, but on your day off you can have a commune.

FADIMAN: Don't you have to destroy The State? It seems logically obvious that this argument cannot continue without your confronting that question. Must you not destroy The State first, or at least at the same time that you are creating the community? I am not now asking whether you would get a better state or a worse one, but must you not destroy the one that serves as the father to which you boys are continually returning? The one which supplies the pipeline from which the communes feed themselves? I'd like to ask Mr. Parker—he's the authority on this.

PARKER: You mean I'm the resident, self-appointed Leninist in the group? Yes, I would agree with Mr. Fadiman. Marc has pointed out that we've talked perpetually in terms of governments and The State, but the economic system with its wage slavery, its forcing us into nine-to-five work schedules, is as enslaving as the government. And, while I see possibilities for manipulating the government, unless we have some really fundamental changes in the economic structure I don't see much. . . .

FADIMAN: Do the other young people support Mr. Parker's statement?

VON SIMSON: Dick and I do not see eye-to-eye on this subject. And I never seem to get an answer to the most naive question that I ask. That is, very simply, who is going to run the airlines and who is going to run the telephones and so forth? This is apparently a very stupid question and is always treated with great contempt. But it's my stumbling block, you see.

FADIMAN: What is your answer?

VON SIMSON: My answer is that these little tribes are just not going to work.

ROSENBLUM: I have difficulty thinking about The State and about society as some kind of monolithic structure, or even as a set of structures. I try and think of it in more dynamic terms. Therefore, I see the overthrow of The State in the form of people who want to change society—that is, people who want to change human relationships by actually doing it. I do not believe the overthrow or destruction of The State is going to come through violence, but through non-violent resistance movements.

ASHMORE: Do you differ with Dick principally on the question of violence?

ROSENBLUM: Yes. Violent revolution tends to be reactionary. . . .

MAYER: Then do you reject compulsion in the new community?

ROSENBLUM: I think there's going to have to be some moral responsibility exercised by individuals in the new society. . . .

MAYER: Is the sense of responsibility going to be conveyed with a club or is it going to come from within?

ROSENBLUM: Ideally, it ought to come from within, from respect for fellow members of the community.

MAYER: It ought to come from within. It doesn't. If nobody will collect the garbage, then what?

ROSENBLUM: Then the society will fall apart. It will deteriorate, it will destroy itself.

SHEINBAUM: Susan has said something important about how change will come, this revolutionary change the young people are thinking about. There is a parallel phenomenon in the labor movement where there is increasing talk about worker control. They want a greater voice in the affairs of corporations. Yesterday's *Wall Street Journal* had a lead article reporting that workers are screwing up the technology because they are starting to show up for four days and not five, even though their union contracts call for five. The point is that much change will come about, not because any group planned for it, or thought it through theoretically,

173

but because of social reaction to certain conditions. These things will occur, and I believe more change will come about this way than through Parker's revolution.

BORGESE: I have been thinking about what Mr. von Simson said, and it doesn't seem to me as convincing as it appeared at first. In Europe there is an emerging philosophy of self-management. Workers control the system under self-management, and then the answer to who is going to run the airlines, or the electricity works is that it will *not* be The State.

VON SIMSON: Well, it certainly won't be these little tribes that everybody is talking about. . . .

BORGESE: My feeling is that Mr. Mayer has overstated the importance of The State. It isn't any longer that important. And a lot of the functions that have to be centralized and universalized are not going to be in the hands of government at all.

MAYER: Here I see myself limping off to Vietnam to get my head shot off and Madame Borgese saying, "Oh come now, The State isn't *that* important." What are you talking about? I'm trying to tell you that The State is all important so long as it will let you do certain things, and compel you to do others.

EBWASSER: What you are saying is true under pres- conditions, as things stand now. I think what Dick ker said was absolutely right and the answer to the stion is, yes, we're going to have to get rid of The te. We are going to have to change political organ- tions. I also think Susan was practically right in talking in terms of nonviolence. But I don't think the crucial question is violence or nonviolence. There are social forces already at work which are going to vastly change our forms of political organization, just as nationalism itself grew up as a response to changing conditions when feudalism declined. This society we have had for a while is coming apart at the seams, and even the middle class in America is beginning to realize that. So we have to change The State, and the evolutionary process seems to me too slow. But I can't support the violent revolution advocated by many of the groups Dick talks about.

ASHMORE: If you are going to attack Mr. Mayer's proposition about The State, which he has stated as eternal truth, don't you have to answer Mr. Fadiman's earlier question as to why you think your pluralistic tribal solution will work now when it never has in the past? The problems surely were easier in a simpler society; almost all the earlier groups were agrarian and could practically expect to support themselves. Today we've got a much more complicated situation. According to Mr. Fadiman, you're simply urging that we try again what never has worked before.

TRIEBWASSER: We have come through the second major revolution in the human experience, the first being the agricultural revolution, the second being the industrial revolution. In the technologically developed society there are new avenues open for creativeness. We do not have to have drudgery. We have for the first time. . . .

FADIMAN: But you have to have organization.

TRIEBWASSER: That's true, you have to have organization. What I am saying is that the present social, political and economic organization is based on pre-technological needs. Now we can vastly revamp it. It isn't a question of getting to a four-day work week, it's a question of changing the whole concept of work.

ASHMORE: I think Mr. Mayer is saying you've also got to have a new man.

TRIEBWASSER: This is, to my mind, one of the crucial points. How do we develop a sense of responsibility in the individual, a feeling for participation in community activities. These are, I think, the crucial questions. . . .

MAYER: Failing to have done that beforehand, will we find it worth having undertaken the tribal adventure?

TRIEBWASSER: No, let me put it this way. I think the revolution, at least the way I conceive it, is in two parts. First, there is a question of getting rid of the injustices in this society as they exist today, that's part of it.

FADIMAN: Within the framework of our present system?

TRIEBWASSER: No, that's the whole point. We can't do that, we have to change the whole system. The second part of the revolution is entertwined with the change in the structure. It's a question of changing the concept of the better way of life. The practical matters Dick and others are bringing up have to be dealt with, but we can't solve our present problems structurally, by altering forms of government or forms of administration. We have to develop attitudinal changes, put human psychology to work to create a working together of people. Since this concept is attitudinal, it is much more difficult to get your hands on it.

MAYER: Yes, indeed. I want to hear Mr. Parker on the subject of Marc's requirement of attitudinal change as a precondition for making a permanent alteration of the horrors of The State I have described in my paper.

PARKER: I don't know if I want to discuss that matter in a particular way. I do want to reiterate the point I've made before: I don't think The State is all-powerful. For example, we're in the process of killing ourselves through pollution in the environment caused by industry, not by The State, and The State seems powerless to stop it. When we talk in these eighteenth century terms about Man versus The State, we continue to overlook this component. The great contribution of nineteenth century social scientists was to make economics an independent science, and it seems to me Mr. Mayer continues to overlook it. Beyond that, I really don't know what to say. I agree that von Simson is right about the necessity of running the airplanes and generating electricity; the system will still have to provide people to do it.

FADIMAN: People operating under what aegis?

PARKER: I think there are ways of conceiving a system in terms of the amount of time people put into it so that, as Marx says, we would not have the present lock-step specialization. We would have to have a power plant, but it might not operate in work shifts made up of straight eight-hour sections.

FADIMAN: What would you say if our present state agreed with you and worked out methods for such amelioration? Would you accept that? I speak now for Dr. Tugwell over there, who is a reformist. It's quite conceivable that within the next ten years our own state will provide the system you have just confronted us with. Then what?

PARKER: Well, I think it would further undercut the possibility of dealing with the concerns I am primarily worried about. I am sure the approach would be another piecemeal. . . .

FADIMAN: It would annoy you?

PARKER: Yes, it would annoy me. But, I'm so preconditioned to losing anyway, it is not going to annoy me significantly.

FADIMAN: A Leninist is preconditioned to eventual victory, not to defeat.

PARKER: I have a horrible dose of Unamuno inside me, you see.

FADIMAN: Ah, I detect it. But I still don't think you have met Mr. von Simson's objections.

PARKER: I think I have. We could go on to talk about airplanes in terms of what I would consider an overgeneration of product or, in this case, an overavailability of aircraft resulting from the competitive character of the market.

ASHMORE: You assume The State continues, and this would mean the airlines would continue to function, under state control or in some other fashion?

PARKER: Right.

MAYER: There are no airlines, Marc, in your society, are there?

TRIEBWASSER: Of course there are. What I'm saying is that you want to provide an airline worker not only with the possibility of being an airline worker, but the possibility of being creative. It is not a question of getting rid of all economic chores. It's a matter of saying that this is only one part of human life, and no one should have to build his life around work—eight hours on the job, eight hours getting ready to go to work and coming back, and eight hours sleeping.

MAYER: You know, our repressive state is already conscious of that fact. It was conscious of it in Plato's time. You're not saying anything new. I haven't heard Mr. Parker tell me how the problem of liberty versus authority is going to disappear, if it is.

PARKER: I don't think it ever is.

MAYER: All right, if it never is, then there's always going to be ultimate compulsion. But you are going to locate power in the hands of what? Of the commune voluntarily organized, in a class of. . . .

PARKER: Well, it would be a combination of all, as it is in the present, not simply in the hands of The State.

179

Ultimate authority doesn't rest in the hands of The State. It rests in a wide variety of social organizations, of which The State is probably the major one, or one of two or three major ones. I think that something like this will probably continue to operate.

MAYER: But you don't want it to continue to operate this way?

PARKER: No. We're going to lose out on this whole structural game, I think, unless somehow we really begin to get sensitive to a change in *ethos*. . . .

MAYER: Hey! You sound like Marc. "Unless somebody gets sensitive to a change of *ethos*." Marc's saying this is a precondition of your revolution, and of his.

PARKER: Well, there is a symbiotic relationship. The conditions existing generate the consciousness as they also generate the need for radical change.

FADIMAN: The new Soviet Man was proclaimed by Mr. Lenin and his successors. He said that at the same time we reconstruct The State we are going to reconstruct the citizen—make a new Soviet man—and boy! Haven't they done it.

PARKER: I think Stalin was enormously insensitive to the whole ethos of Marxism, don't you?

FADIMAN: I think he was an s. o. b.; I don't think there is anything else to be said about him.

PARKER: Stalin was totally insensitive, that's my point.

I think he was totally insensitive, and I am going to lose any argument that turns on the example of the Soviet Union, which I don't choose to defend.

FADIMAN: I'm not being a Red-baiter, Mr. Parker. That's not the point. The point is that whenever you try to create consciously the new man, you seemingly must also create equally consciously a new state apparatus to foster him and eventually control him and give him orders. At least that's the history so far.

MAYER: There is more to it than that. In this Marxist dream of the new man you are attempting to establish a system which will bring him forward, not merely control him—a system which in effect will produce him. You don't just strike the shackles off the old man. You have to provide the kind of education and the kind of culture that will make men new.

TRIEBWASSER: We are doing that, I think, to a limited extent. I was at the Woodstock Festival in White Lake, New York. This has been reported well in the papers— somewhere in the neighborhood of three hundred thousand people in a place supposed to accommodate a hundred thousand, with the worst conditions of discomfort I've ever seen: muddy fields to sleep in, food in short supply, and so forth. And yet a great feeling developed there. Everyone was "doing his own thing" but there was a great feeling that everyone around you was your brother. With all the pot smoking that went on and everything else, there was a tremendous consideration for other people. The police and the local people said that this was the most courteous bunch of youngsters they had ever seen.

VON SIMSON: This is supposed to be a big, red-hot deal for the younger generation? I quite agree that if some young people go off for a weekend together and get stoned out of their minds they can have a lovely time. But it's a hell of a long way from that kind of outing to saying that they can run any kind of society whatsoever. When the outing at Woodstock was over they all went home to have their showers and go back to their jobs or back to school. This is hardly a telling example of the new man.

FADIMAN: If the Woodstock convocation had been denied any avenue of publicity whatsoever—that is, if electronics hadn't helped build up the event—would you have had the same feeling?

TRIEBWASSER: I wouldn't have had the same feeling because without the electronics I couldn't have heard the music. I am not afraid of technology. I want to use technology to help most human needs—I was born in the post-technological era. . . .

ASHMORE: I understand that the young man who put up the money for Woodstock lost hundreds of thousands of dollars because the fences went down and he couldn't collect the admission fee.

MAYER: And it didn't matter.

ASHMORE: Maybe not, but some accounts I've read suggested that there would have been great trouble had the promoter said, O.K., if you don't pay the admission fee I'm going to stop the music. Some of the musicians said they were afraid to stop playing. Do you think the mood of love would have prevailed had the young people been denied anything they wanted?

WHEELER: I'd like to express a different order of concern. I have a feeling that in describing their revolution the young people are right historically. That is, I believe they are going to succeed, or at least that their revolution will exist long enough to create enough communes and confrontational organizations, demonstrations, movements, that they will make a very, very serious dent in the established order. I think that dent probably will be so severe that it may well threaten to bring the established order to its knees. Now, my concern is that, if history is any guide, this kind of thing has happened many times in the past, and what it succeeded in doing was to introduce novelty into the established order, but novelty of a very undesirable type. This kind of movement stimulated the appearance of reaction and repression and dictatorship.

In the revolutionary movement today there is an unfortunate diremption between the activists, the people who are making the confrontation, and the people who perhaps have it within their power to trigger reaction. These people may not be too attractive to the revolutionaries, but they have their hands on the innovations in software that go along with the technological order that Marc is going to rely upon; they are the radical social scientists, the radical mathematicians, the radical ecologists, the people who might conceivably provide the necessary utopian alternatives that would be required if the dictatorial and totalitarian implications of revolutionary confrontation are to be avoided.

It seems to me the most pressing item on the agenda requires the revolutionaries not only to perfect the communes and develop new modes of life for self-expression and self-development, but at the same time to establish some kind of liaison with the radical social scientists who might find ways to provide for the airplanes and the other technological necessities they have symbolized in this discussion—to meet those needs so that they can be humane, not totalitarian features of the post-revolutionary future.

ROSENBLUM: I agree with Mr. Wheeler. We have the example of what happened in Italy and Germany before World War II, where there was a strong youth movement which took on communitarian or communal form. These young people were far outside the mainstream of German society, disillusioned with conventional politics and reform. The *Wandervögel* emphasized the charismatic leader, mysticism, and the *volk* mentality. They stressed changing human relations and the individual instead of existing political and social institutions, and because of this they were very easily exploited. . . .

FADIMAN: They played right into Hitler's hands themselves, and made themselves available for extermination. . . .

ROSENBLUM: Right. I am worried because I think there is a similar tendency today among young people. A lot of the communes that are now appearing are really outside the mainstream of society. I agree that there must be liaison and effective communication between young people who are trying to work for the revolution, and the people who have the technology and the skills.

SHEINBAUM: I agree, and at the same time I have to

make the point that you may be talking about an unrealistic solution. The communes may work for some people but, given the nature of society, it is unrealistic to think they would inspire very many. In terms of Woodstock, for example, there's also a hell of a lot of camaraderie in the military, the real camaraderie of shared experience and common hardship.

MAYER: Yes, the characteristic difference obviously is that Woodstock was totally unorganized, while the army is totally organized; the army endures like Mr. Wheeler's Pilgrim Fathers, while Woodstock runs for a weekend; and the answer to who collects the garbage in Woodstock is that the whole thing would have fallen apart first thing Monday if the people who went to Woodstock had come from anywhere else in the world, where they all had to be at work at 8:00 a.m. Monday morning. In a less affluent society there wouldn't have been anyone left behind to collect the garbage.

ASHMORE: I seem to hear a contradiction in the statements of Marc and Susan that does not exist in what Dick Parker has said. There seems to be an absolute commitment to a kind of ultimate individual freedom, and at the same time a commitment to some concept of collective action through community. I don't think that the gap is bridged by your argument for voluntarism, Marc.

MAYER: And what if the community is the United States of America, and you are not allowed to pull out?

TRIEBWASSER: Are you talking about things as they are now, or things the way I would like to see them organized? I believe we can develop a concept of interdependence so that we do not have to rely on the authority of The State to assure community, rather relying on the very essence of human nature. It would not be The State telling me that I have to stay in the community, but my own human nature.

MAYER: Your self-fulfillment requires brotherhood, is this what you mean?

TRIEBWASSER: Yes it does. Not having a system or a God to look up to, I find I have to begin all my sentences with "I" instead of "he" or "it." I feel very much alone, and I find that the only way of surviving on this planet is at least to make the "I" part of a "we."

MAYER: But how big or small is this brotherhood? How inclusive or non-inclusive? You're going to belong to a tribe. Suppose I belong to a rival tribe?

TRIEBWASSER: The answer is in the formulation I use, which I hope isn't hackneyed. It is a matter of universal concern within ethnic contexts, communal contexts.

MAYER: Universal?

TRIEBWASSER: The concern is for all men. I disagree with Susan about world community, because I think we have to work with much smaller groups. But the concern is universal, the statement is that I will work for this universal good through my own community. It's a matter of methodology; I cannot relate to two hundred million people, but I can relate to maybe a few thousand, in an overlapping social sub-structure. There are various ways of getting from the individual to the world.

MAYER: If we get into a dispute over hunting rights, are you going to go with your tribe, or are you going to say these are all my brothers, and for hunting purposes we are all one tribe?

TRIEBWASSER: The question of how to adjudicate between conflicting communities is important, and very difficult. Where Roman jurisprudence, and later on Christendom, made a mistake was in the belief that adjudication of such conflicts requires universal law. One keeps disputes on a certain level, and treats them in a dynamic context.

ASHMORE: You have said you prefer a nonpolitical approach, but you're talking in political terms now, so I would like to ask a political question. I gather you are talking about some ultimate form of participational democracy. Does this mean you would find any kind of representational democracy of the type we are accustomed to totally foreign to your tribal concept?

TRIEBWASSER: There are certain decisions which will have to be made on a "national" level, and some system would have to be worked out to have those handled by representatives of the various communities. However, I believe decision-making at this level can be minimal, dealing only with service functions, leaving most decisions to be made locally with total participation by a process of consensual democracy.

WHEELER: Marc said he disagreed with Susan in her view on world organization. I have the feeling that she's on the right track. The only way you can counterbalance this state that you are in trouble with would be under some kind of world order.

ROSENBLUM: I personally feel that nationalism for some countries is obsolete, and so is the concept of The State. But I am concerned about the problem that still exists in the Third World. We still have people there who are in a colonial situation; for that matter we have people in the United States who feel they are in a colonial situation, caught by poverty and powerlessness. For those people, our talk about abundance and affluence is irrelevant. And while I feel that for some countries it is essential to move toward world government, or identification with world community, this doesn't relate to the problem of those people who are hungry.

MAYER: And those are most of the people in the world. Are they interested in liberty or security?

ROSENBLUM: They are interested in survival.

MAYER: And will they give up liberty for survival?

ROSENBLUM: Probably.

MAYER: And will a rich American also give up liberty for survival?

ROSENBLUM: I don't know.

ASHMORE: Susan, you have said that you have doubts about democracy, meaning, I assume, the kind of democracy we profess in this country. So, pursuing the question I asked Marc, as you see the development of your theory of community, does it require a participation, or consensual form? Does it have room for representative democracy, for decision-making by even an idealized version of the elective processes we employ in this country now?

ROSENBLUM: I feel that given the crisis we are faced with in this society and in the world we have to make explicit, individual value judgements, and that majority opinion can no longer be considered a sacred concept. I know I may be talking about some kind of benevolent dictatorship, but I feel there is a certain standard of morality that must be universally applied. . . .

ASHMORE: Could you accept even the most benevolent dictatorship within your concept of a commune? Could it be run by a totally benevolent dictator?

ROSENBLUM: I haven't decided about the ramifications of that issue. At this point I would probably say no, if that authority were backed up by violence and force.

TUGWELL: I don't think we discussed Mr. Mayer's topic. He kept trying to make us discuss it, but we didn't get to it. We couldn't because nobody will admit that The State exists.

ASHMORE: I think Mr. Parker, at least, has agreed that you've got to have The State.

BARTLETT: The question was raised whether or not the proposal for a pluralistic tribal society would be theo-

189

retically compatible with technology. That question was never solved.

WHEELER: Wouldn't you say it was addressed, and a possible solution offered, in terms of some kind of liaison between radical software technologists and radical activists?

ASHMORE: Isn't there an enduring theoretical question that Mr. Mayer dealt with through a parade of theoretical concepts reaching all the way from Athens to yesterday's Supreme Court decisions—that arising from the ancient conflict between Man and The State? I thought Mr. Mayer was trying to say to Marc and the others that they have to face this question, whether they propose to meet the technological age with a return to tribalism, or follow Mr. Parker to the barricades.

TUGWELL: I have been looking for an opportunity to say that The State is after all the creation of man.

MAYER: I think that's a fiction.

TUGWELL: The State exists. It is the creation of man. Why can't we do anything with it we like? We have all this technology and all this affluence to do it with.

MAYER: Has the technology liberated us as individuals? Has it in fact liberated us . . . ?

TUGWELL: No, because we haven't managed it.

MAYER: Is there something inherent in it that keeps us from managing it?

TUGWELL: Personally, I don't think there is, except that it has its own laws. Those require that technology must be big. It has to be comprehensive. And that probably means the tribes and the communes are impossible.

WHEELER: Let me try to summarize. We might state the problem Mr. Mayer wants solved in the following terms: In the good old days the role of politics was believed to be the creation of The State; in using politics to create The State, we assumed that we also would create the conditions of liberty. Now it turns out that this appears to have been a wrong lead, largely because of the irreversible requirements of the technological society. So, what we have to do now is reverse our traditional ideas of politics. In the new view, politics will not be concerned with creating The State, as of old. On the contrary, it will be concerned primarily with the destruction of The State, at least the classical nation-state definition. The new technological environment is tied to the old form of The State. This means that in the future we may have to regard The State, or rather its successor, as a public utility, a service facility; something like a public power company. Then the functions of The State will become services one subscribes to rather than processes one creates through politics. So we turn politics away from state-creating, and convert it into a pluralist community-creating endeavor. Politics reverses itself—instead of being directed up to a monolith it is directed back to the community. Is this in line with your thinking?

MAYER: Santa Barbara, 1969—when and where we finally discovered that politics is not the architectonic science. . . .

Statement of Ownership, Management and Circulation (Act of October 23, 1962; Section 4369, Title 39, United States Code)
(1) Date of Filing, September 10, 1969; (2) Title of Publication, A CENTER OCCASIONAL PAPER; (3) Frequency of Issue: Bi-monthly — (omits August); (4) Location of Known Office of Publication: 2056 Eucalyptus Hill Road, Santa Barbara, California 93103; (5) Location of the Headquarters or General Business Offices of the Publishers: same as above.
(6) Names and Addresses of Publisher, Editor, and Managing Editor: Publisher, The Fund for the Republic, Inc., 2056 Eucalyptus Hill Road, Santa Barbara, California 93103; Editor, John Cogley, 2056 Eucalyptus Hill Road, Santa Barbara, California 93103; Managing Editor, Donald McDonald, 2056 Eucalyptus Hill Road, Santa Barbara, California 93103.
(7) Owner: The Fund for the Republic, Inc., 2056 Eucalyptus Hill Road, Santa Barbara, California 93103; no stockholders.
(8) Known Bondholders, Mortgagees, and Other Security Holders Owning or Holding 1 Percent or More of Total Amount of Bonds, Mortgages or Other Securities: None.
(9) For completion by Nonprofit Organizations Authorized to Mail at Special Rates (Section 132.-122, Postal Manual): The purpose, function, and nonprofit status of this organization and the exempt status for Federal income tax purposes have not changed during preceding 12 months.
(10) Extent and Nature of Circulation:

		Average no. copies each issue during preceding 12 months	Single issue nearest to filing date
[A]	Total No. Copies Printed (net press run)	95,115	110,688
[B]	Paid Circulation		
	1. Sales through Dealers and Carriers, Street Vendors, and Counter Sales	742	99
	2. Mail Subscriptions	87,366	100,927
[C]	Total Paid Circulation	88,108	101,926
[D]	Free Distribution (including samples) by Mail, Carrier, or Other Means	820	706
[E]	Total Distribution (Sum of C and D)	88,928	102,632
[F]	Office Use, Left-Over, Unaccounted, Spoiled after Printing	6,187	8,056
[G]	Total (Sum of E and F — should equal net press run shown in A)	95,115	110,688

I certify that the statements made by me above are correct and complete.

Peter Tagger, *Business Manager*